Learning Underscore.js

Explore the Underscore.js library using a test-driven
development approach

Alex Pop

BIRMINGHAM - MUMBAI

Learning Underscore.js

First published: October 2015

Production reference: 1261015

Published by Packt Publishing Ltd.
Livery Place
35 Livery Street
Birmingham B3 2PB, UK.

ISBN 978-1-78439-381-6

www.packtpub.com

Credits

Author
Alex Pop

Reviewers
Craig Davis
Pavel Tkachenko
Jitendra Zaa

Commissioning Editor
Dipika Gaonkar

Acquisition Editors
Indrajit Das
Rebecca Pedley

Content Development Editor
Divij Kotian

Technical Editor
Siddhi Rane

Copy Editor
Janbal Dharmaraj

Project Coordinator
Nikhil Nair

Proofreader
Safis Editing

Indexer
Hemangini Bari

Production Coordinator
Komal Ramchandani

Cover Work
Komal Ramchandani

About the Author

Alex Pop is a professional software developer with 14 years of experience in building applications for various platforms and technologies.

He has worked for ISVs, building enterprise resource planning applications, a content management system, and insurance and financial software products, and is currently working in the higher education sector as a web application developer.

He is the author of *Learning AngularJS for .NET Developers, Packt Publishing*. His developer blog at http://alexvpop.blogspot.co.uk/ contains technical articles about .NET, JavaScript, and various software engineering topics.

I would like to thank my wife and daughter for their support and understanding.

About the Reviewers

Craig Davis is a software engineer with a 20-year history in the web industry. He works at Help Scout, an organization that helps people bring personalized e-mail support to the enterprise. He has been a technical editor for many programming books and is proud to contribute to multiple open source projects. He is a competitive cyclist and runner and lives in New Mexico with his wife and their dog.

Pavel Tkachenko is an inspired self-taught computer wizard. Since childhood, he has had a passion for designing and developing websites and maintaining complex server architectures. He has created a number of original tools, such as HTMLki, Sqobot, and Sqimitive, to tackle common problems in a new way. He is also the founder of the Russian Laravel community and an active member of Russian publication networks such as Habrahabr.ru.

He has been freelancing since 2009, working on all sorts of websites built around PHP, Rails, Python, JavaScript, and MySQL. He used to lead his own team as well as work on his own. His views are often unconventional, but that's what allows him to work on high-profile projects with a custom approach. You can contact him via his page at http://proger.me.

Jitendra Zaa is Salesforce MVP with more than 6 years of experience in web technologies and cloud platforms. He is a manager at Cognizant technology solutions.

You can follow him @JitendraZaa or at his website http://jitendrazaa.com/.

Writing technical blog articles, learning new programming languages and frameworks, and sharing knowledge with others are some of his hobbies.

His experience and projects normally include Salesforce, Java, C#, ASP.Net, JIRA, and PHP-based applications.

Other books he has reviewed include *Force.com Enterprise Architecture*, *Developing Applications with Salesforce Chatter*, and *Visualforce Development Cookbook*, all by Packt Publishing. Right now, he is writing a book on design patterns in Salesforce with Packt Publishing.

I would like to thank my mom, dad, my wife, Minal, and our adorable son, Rudra, for all their support, time, and above all for the motivation to go on.

www.PacktPub.com

Support files, eBooks, discount offers, and more

For support files and downloads related to your book, please visit www.PacktPub.com.

Did you know that Packt offers eBook versions of every book published, with PDF and ePub files available? You can upgrade to the eBook version at www.PacktPub.com and as a print book customer, you are entitled to a discount on the eBook copy. Get in touch with us at service@packtpub.com for more details.

At www.PacktPub.com, you can also read a collection of free technical articles, sign up for a range of free newsletters and receive exclusive discounts and offers on Packt books and eBooks.

https://www2.packtpub.com/books/subscription/packtlib

Do you need instant solutions to your IT questions? PacktLib is Packt's online digital book library. Here, you can search, access, and read Packt's entire library of books.

Why subscribe?

- Fully searchable across every book published by Packt
- Copy and paste, print, and bookmark content
- On demand and accessible via a web browser

Free access for Packt account holders

If you have an account with Packt at www.PacktPub.com, you can use this to access PacktLib today and view 9 entirely free books. Simply use your login credentials for immediate access.

Table of Contents

Preface

Over the last few years, JavaScript has emerged as one the most popular programming languages, expanding its reach from its original browser environment to server runtimes, databases, and to mobile, embedded, or desktop applications. The sixth edition of its specification ECMAScript 2015 (ES6) was a major milestone that brought JavaScript features in line with other popular programming languages. The community and the browser vendors stepped up their efforts to support ES6, and we should see full support for the standard across multiple JavaScript engines as soon as early 2016. The future of JavaScript beyond ES6 looks very promising as its standardization effort aims to release a new specification every year.

In summer 2015, JavaScript was the most popular language used on the GitHub repository hosting service and had the biggest number of packages compared to all other languages. This change in popularity was made possible by an intense process of creation and refinement of libraries and frameworks alongside an improvement in development standards and practices throughout the JavaScript community. One of these modern JavaScript libraries is jQuery, the most popular browser library, which was a great facilitator in speeding up the adoption of common web standards across browser engines. Similarly, at least in impact, the Underscore library brought uniformity and functional programming features to JavaScript while bridging the gap between client and server environments.

Underscore represents a model of code quality and community involvement that other libraries should try to emulate, and many libraries were inspired or built upon Underscore. Throughout this book, Underscore proved to be the perfect vehicle to explore programming concepts that apply to any type of application. It is also a great example for the concept of universal JavaScript where the same code can be executed in multiple environments. For a JavaScript developer, Underscore is the JavaScript-based library that can be used to create code that runs everywhere or as a foundation for adopting a functional programming style.

JavaScript has become an important language in enterprise software development with the adoption of the Node.js runtime by companies such as Microsoft, IBM, and Intel to name just a few. The considerable rise in popularity of single page application frameworks, such as Backbone.js, AngularJS, React, and many others, means that developers are writing more complex JavaScript code with an increased effort in managing the increase in complexity. Adopting standards such as ES6 and using Underscore or similar libraries should help in coping with the challenges of the rapidly and continuously changing industry.

What this book covers

Chapter 1, Getting Started with Underscore.js, introduces you to Underscore and explains the main problems addressed by the library together with a quick introduction to functional programming. This chapter describes some of the concepts and patterns that are used by Underscore or are helpful when using Underscore. The final part is a walkthrough to set up the development environment used throughout the book with a starter example.

Chapter 2, Using Underscore.js with Collections, explores the Underscore functionality for collections by example and explains some of the concepts related to these areas — scope resolution and execution context, map/reduce, and functional programming concepts.

Chapter 3, Using Underscore.js with Arrays, Objects, and Functions, looks at functionality for arrays, objects, and functions and builds upon the concepts and functions introduced in the previous chapter. In the functions section, you will learn how to manipulate function scopes and arguments and why this is an important aspect of JavaScript programming in general.

Chapter 4, Programming Paradigms with Underscore.js, expands on the concepts and practices of functional programming to solve common programming problems. The chapter starts with a differentiation between object-oriented programming and functional programming. It continues by exploring examples of functional programming with Underscore.

Chapter 5, Using Underscore.js in the Browser, on the Server, and with the Database, is about using Underscore in specific contexts, starting with the browser environment, closely followed by Node.js server-side applications or libraries. You will then learn how to use Underscore with databases such as MongoDB and PostgreSQL, which can execute JavaScript to query data.

Chapter 6, Related Underscore.js Libraries and ECMAScript Standards, discusses advanced topics such as the link between Underscore and JavaScript standards, libraries that augment or can even replace Underscore, with a focus on taking advantage of the new ECMAScript 2015 (ES6) features.

Chapter 7, Underscore.js Build Automation and Code Reusability, introduces a build automation solution together with strategies to reuse Underscore based code between different application hosts.

What you need for this book

You need to have the Node.js runtime installed and it is available at `https://nodejs.org/`. Details on how to install it can be found in *Chapter 1, Getting Started with Underscore.js*.

All the code in this book can be edited in any text editor or IDE that you are familiar with and has support for the JavaScript language.

Who this book is for

This book is for developers with fundamental JavaScript knowledge who want to use modern JavaScript libraries to advance their programming skills. Underscore is one of the most important libraries you should be familiar with and the book will help you achieve this goal by going through its fundamentals and using it in a wide variety of contexts. This book should be relevant to anyone who:

- Is interested in building web applications, single-page web applications or JavaScript-based desktop, mobile, or embedded applications
- Wants to use Node.js to build web applications or web services
- Wants to work with databases such as MongoDB or PostgreSQL and leverage their JavaScript support

Conventions

In this book, you will find a number of text styles that distinguish between different kinds of information. Here are some examples of these styles and an explanation of their meaning.

Code words in text, database table names, folder names, filenames, file extensions, pathnames, dummy URLs, user input, and Twitter handles are shown as follows: "We just need to open the `SpecRunner.html` file in a browser and we should see this output."

A block of code is set as follows:

```
var peopleWithAwardAge = _.map(people, function(person){
  return {
    name: person.name,
    awardAge: person.awardYear - person.birthYear
  }
});
```

When we wish to draw your attention to a particular part of a code block, the relevant lines or items are set in bold:

```
var peopleWithAwardAge = _.map(people, function(person){
  return {
    name: person.name,
    awardAge: person.awardYear - person.birthYear
  }
});
```

Any command-line input or output is written as follows:

```
npm install -g bower
```

New terms and **important words** are shown in bold. Words that you see on the screen, for example, in menus or dialog boxes, appear in the text like this: "Executing the following line in a Command Prompt with administrator privileges (opened using the **Run as administrator** option)."

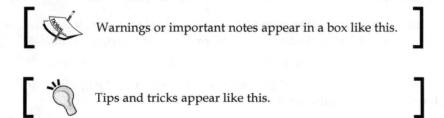

> [Warnings or important notes appear in a box like this.]

> [Tips and tricks appear like this.]

Reader feedback

Feedback from our readers is always welcome. Let us know what you think about this book—what you liked or disliked. Reader feedback is important for us as it helps us develop titles that you will really get the most out of.

To send us general feedback, simply e-mail feedback@packtpub.com, and mention the book's title in the subject of your message.

If there is a topic that you have expertise in and you are interested in either writing or contributing to a book, see our author guide at www.packtpub.com/authors.

Customer support

Now that you are the proud owner of a Packt book, we have a number of things to help you to get the most from your purchase.

Downloading the example code

You can download the example code files from your account at http://www.packtpub.com for all the Packt Publishing books you have purchased. If you purchased this book elsewhere, you can visit http://www.packtpub.com/support and register to have the files e-mailed directly to you.

Errata

Although we have taken every care to ensure the accuracy of our content, mistakes do happen. If you find a mistake in one of our books—maybe a mistake in the text or the code—we would be grateful if you could report this to us. By doing so, you can save other readers from frustration and help us improve subsequent versions of this book. If you find any errata, please report them by visiting http://www.packtpub.com/submit-errata, selecting your book, clicking on the **Errata Submission Form** link, and entering the details of your errata. Once your errata are verified, your submission will be accepted and the errata will be uploaded to our website or added to any list of existing errata under the Errata section of that title.

To view the previously submitted errata, go to https://www.packtpub.com/books/content/support and enter the name of the book in the search field. The required information will appear under the **Errata** section.

Piracy

Piracy of copyrighted material on the Internet is an ongoing problem across all media. At Packt, we take the protection of our copyright and licenses very seriously. If you come across any illegal copies of our works in any form on the Internet, please provide us with the location address or website name immediately so that we can pursue a remedy.

Please contact us at copyright@packtpub.com with a link to the suspected pirated material.

We appreciate your help in protecting our authors and our ability to bring you valuable content.

Questions

If you have a problem with any aspect of this book, you can contact us at questions@packtpub.com, and we will do our best to address the problem.

1
Getting Started with Underscore.js

This chapter introduces you to Underscore and explains the main problems addressed by this library together with a quick introduction to functional programming. The chapter describes some of the concepts and patterns that are used by Underscore or are helpful when using Underscore. The final part is a walkthrough to set up the development environment used throughout the book.

The topics covered in this chapter are as follows:

- Why Underscore
- Getting started with Underscore by example
- Key Underscore functions
- Functional programming fundamentals
- Useful patterns and practices for JavaScript applications targeting ECMAScript 5
- Setting up a development workflow to explore Underscore
- Testing JavaScript code with Jasmine

The chapter assumes that you know JavaScript programming fundamentals and how to create basic web pages using HTML, CSS, and jQuery.

The source code for all the examples from this chapter is also hosted online on GitHub at `https://github.com/popalexandruvasile/underscorejs-examples/tree/master/getting-started`.

Why Underscore

In the last couple of years, the JavaScript programming language has extended its reach dramatically. While initially it was a browser-based scripting language, it is now used in server-side applications via platforms such as Node.js or in mobile and desktop applications via frameworks such as PhoneGap and Node-Webkit. Database engines such as MongoDB and PostgreSQL also use JavaScript, and this makes it possible to write an application using the same programming language throughout all its layers and components. Another significant change that raised the importance of JavaScript was the emergence of libraries and frameworks that targeted the browser as an application platform. Libraries such as jQuery enabled cross-browser HTML element manipulation, among other features, and frameworks such as Backbone.js facilitated building single page applications.

 A single page application (also known as **SPA**) has the user interface rendering and navigation happening in the browser rather than on the server.

The library presented in this book is called Underscore and provides an extensive set of functions that simplify and enhance handling of JavaScript objects, arrays, and functions. It accomplishes this by providing missing functional programming features to JavaScript. By using Underscore JavaScript gains a better level of usability that makes coding easier and more expressive on a similar level to other general purpose programming languages.

Version 1.0 of Underscore was launched in 2010 around the time when single page applications started to gain more ground. Underscore is used in Backbone.js as both have the same author, and after its launch it has become one of the most popular JavaScript libraries. At the time of writing this book, Underscore has reached version 1.8.3, which will be the version used throughout all examples.

Underscore is representative of a good JavaScript utility library as it provides solutions for a specific problem domain rather than being a catchall utility. It also has very good online documentation (including annotated source code) that is available at `http://underscorejs.org/`, which is another distinctive attribute of a good software library. This book will explore Underscore by presenting a series of more involved examples than the ones provided with its library documentation.

To understand why Underscore is so popular, we need to discuss the **ECMAScript 5 (ES5)** specification and what it meant for JavaScript as a programming language. Technically, JavaScript is a specific implementation of an open language specification called ECMAScript. The current version of this specification was finalized at the end of 2009 and is known as ECMAScript 5 (or ECMAScript 5.1 to be very specific). This version added functionality for the built-in JavaScript objects, `Array` and `Object`, included new functional features, and improved the meta-programming story among other changes. Soon after its release, it started to be adopted by all major browsers, including Internet Explorer from version 9. There was still a large number of users relying on browsers such as Internet Explorer 6, 7, and 8 that were unlikely to upgrade too quickly to Internet Explorer 9 compared to users of browsers such as Mozilla Firefox and Google Chrome that had faster release and upgrade cycles. As Underscore provided support for some of the functionality introduced by ECMAScript 5, this made it a useful library for web applications targeting older browsers such as Internet Explorer 8, and for developers that wanted to write code that was based on ES5 without worrying about browser support. Although ES5 support is important, this is just a small feature of Underscore compared to the rest of its features.

All of this book's examples assume that they are executed against a JavaScript version that is ES5 compliant. All the examples can be executed on Windows, Mac OS X, and Linux, and we will mainly target Google Chrome and Mozilla Firefox that are the most popular cross platform browsers (although you should not have issues running the examples in other browsers).

Technically, Underscore is not directly compatible with ES5 starting from version 1.7.0, and we will discuss more about standards compliance in *Chapter 6, Related Underscore.js Libraries and ECMAScript Standards*.

ES 5 support for older browsers should be provided through a library targeting this feature exclusively such as **es5-shim**. This library is available at `https://github.com/es-shims/es5-shim`, where you can find more details about its features.

Getting started with Underscore by example

The best way to introduce Underscore is with examples. We will target the same problem and solve it first using plain JavaScript that is ES5 compliant followed by a couple of Underscore-based solutions.

The ECMAScript 5 starter example

The examples presented in this chapter are hosted in web pages, and they can be executed by opening the index.html example file in your preferred web browser.

We start with a dataset that contains various bicycles and each one has a specific type. We want to process the dataset and get a count of bicycles for each bicycle type. The dataset is represented by an array of bicycle objects created using the object literal notation:

```
var bicycles = [{
    name: "A fast bike",
    type: "Road Bike"
}, {
    name: "An even faster bike",
    type: "Road Bike"
}, {
    name: "A springy bike",
    type: "Mountain Bike"
}, {
    name: "A springier bike",
    type: "Mountain Bike"
}, {
    name: "An all-terain bike",
    type: "Mountain Bike"
}, {
    name: "A classy bike",
    type: "Urban Bike"
}, {
    name: "A modern bike",
    type: "Urban Bike"
}, {
    name: "A blue bike",
    type: "Children Bike"
}, {
    name: "A pink bike",
    type: "Children Bike"
}, {
    name: "A noisy bike",
    type: "Children Bike"
}, {
    name: "A clown bike",
    type: "Children Bike"
}];
```

Next, we will define a function that processes the dataset and creates an array of objects that contains the count of bicycles for a specific bicycle type:

```
var getBicyclesCountPerType = function() {
  var bicyclesCountPerType = [];
  bicycles.forEach(function(bicycle) {
    var isExistingType = false;
    bicyclesCountPerType.forEach(function(typeCount) {
      if (typeCount.type === bicycle.type) {
        typeCount.count += 1;
        isExistingType = true;
      }
    });
    if (!isExistingType) {
      bicyclesCountPerType.push({
        type: bicycle.type,
        count: 1
      });
    }
  });
  return bicyclesCountPerType;
};
```

The first highlighted function `forEach` is ES5 specific and enumerates the values of an array while executing a function for each element in the array. The `forEach` function is defined against `Array.prototype`, so it will be available to any `Array` instance.

The final code snippet for the first example relies on jQuery to append the results for each bicycle type as HTML content:

```
$(document).ready(function() {
  var outputContent = "There are " + bicycles.length + "
  bicycles:"
  var results = getBicyclesCountPerType();
  results.forEach(function(typeCount) {
    outputContent += "<br />";
```

```
    outputContent += " - " + typeCount.count + " of type: " +
    typeCount.type;
  });

  $("#output").html(outputContent);
});
```

Notice how we use `forEach` again to enumerate the final results. You can explore the example in the `starter-example-with-ECMAScript5` folder from the source code for this chapter. In order to run this example, you need to open the `index.html` file in your preferred web browser. The example can also be executed directly at `http://bit.ly/1WLzHuS`.

You can view the example output in this screenshot:

Example output:
There are 11 bicycles:
- 2 of type: Road Bike
- 3 of type: Mountain Bike
- 2 of type: Urban Bike
- 4 of type: Children Bike

The Underscore find starter example

In the previous example, we used two-nested `forEach` calls, and this approach seems inefficient under closer scrutiny. You cannot break a `forEach` loop, which means that you cannot stop after you processed the specific elements that were targeted. The second nested `forEach` call only needs to process a target element from the list rather than iterating the full list every time. Fortunately, Underscore has a function called `find` that iterates an array and stops when an element matching a specific criteria is found.

To use Underscore, we need to add a reference to a hosted version of the library in the `head` element of the example web page:

```
<script src="http://cdnjs.cloudflare.com/ajax/
libs/underscore.js/1.8.3/underscore.js"></script>
```

In the first example, we changed the function `getBicyclesCountPerType()` to use the Underscore `find` function:

```
var getBicyclesCountPerType = function() {
```

```
var bicyclesCountPerType = [];
bicycles.forEach(function(bicycle) {
  var currentTypeCount = _.find(bicyclesCountPerType,
  function(typeCount){
    return typeCount.type === bicycle.type;
  });
  if (currentTypeCount) {
    currentTypeCount.count += 1;
  }
  else
  {
    bicyclesCountPerType.push({
      type: bicycle.type,
      count: 1
    });
  }
});
return bicyclesCountPerType;
};
```

The code is terser and more efficient thanks to the `find` function, while the rest of the example remains unchanged. You can explore the full example in the `starter-example-with-underscore.find` folder from the source code for this chapter or by running it directly at `http://bit.ly/1U7dVO4`.

All Underscore functions are usually accessed through the Underscore global object named `_`. This name can be changed if it conflicts with other global variable names, and we will explore how to do this in *Chapter 4, Programming Paradigms with Underscore.js*. We will stick with the default Underscore global object name for most of the examples.

The full signature of the `find` function is `_.find(list, predicate, [context])`. This function accepts an array or an object as its first parameter `list` followed by a function parameter `predicate` that will be executed against each element of the array or against each property value of the object passed as the first parameter. The second parameter function `predicate` accepts an array element or an object property value and should return a Boolean value. If the return value is `true`, the `_.find()` function will stop iterating and will return the array element or the property value from the current position. The last optional parameter `context` is rarely used in this book and will be covered later on when we discuss scopes and the value of the `this` object. The `find` function signature was briefly explored here as it is used extensively in Underscore and subsequently in the rest of the examples.

In ES6, there is also a find function defined against Array.prototype that can be used as an alternative. We will discuss this function and other similar ECMAScript 6 functions in *Chapter 6, Related Underscore.js Libraries and ECMAScript Standards.*

The Underscore countBy starter example

The previous example introduced Underscore as an incremental improvement compared to the example before that. Among Underscore's 100+ functions, there is one that can replace the getBicyclesCountPerType() function completely and significantly reduce the number of lines of code. This function is countBy and its signature is _.countBy(list, iteratee, [context]). While its signature is similar with the one for the find function, the second function parameter iteratee is expected to return a string value representing a key for the iterated item. The key is used to group different elements of an array or different object property values depending on the list parameter type.

The countBy function returns an object with properties that have names taken from the keys supplied by the iteratee function. The value of such a property is the count of items from the list parameter that share the current property name as key.

The getBicyclesCountPerType() function invocation can be completely replaced with the _.countBy() function invocation:

```
var result = _.countBy(bicycles, function(bicycle){
    return bicycle.type;
});
```

The result object value has the following JSON representation:

```
{
    "Road Bike": 2,
    "Mountain Bike": 3,
    "Urban Bike": 2,
    "Children Bike": 4
}
```

The code tasked with displaying the example output needs to be changed accordingly. Instead of manipulating the array returned by the `getBicyclesCountPerType()` function it should manipulate the `result` object properties. We will use another Underscore function `_.pairs()`, which converts object properties to an array of elements where each element is a property name and value pair. Such a pair is a two-dimensional array itself, and you can see how it is declared and referenced in the highlighted sections from the following example:

```
$(document).ready(function() {
  var outputContent = "There are " + bicycles.length + "
  bicycles:"
  var result = _.countBy(bicycles, function(bicycle) {
    return bicycle.type;
  });
  _.pairs(result).forEach(function(typeCountPair) {
    var key = typeCountPair[0];
    var value = typeCountPair[1];
    outputContent += "<br />";
    outputContent += " - " + value + " of type: " + key;
  });
  $("#output").html(outputContent);
});
```

We have now dramatically reduced the size of the initial example by using Underscore functions while maintaining the same functionality. You can explore the full example in the `starter-example-with-underscore.countBy` folder from the source code for this chapter or by running it directly at `http://bit.ly/1JdNwc6`.

We started with one example that uses ES5 functions, followed by one that uses an Underscore function that is also an ES6 function. The final example uses another Underscore specific function that provides a higher level of data manipulation compared to built in JavaScript functions. You should find a lot more Underscore examples of this kind throughout the book.

Key Underscore functions

Out of the many Underscore functions, there are a couple that deserve special attention as they provide a good introduction to a range of similar functions. These functions are essential when processing data, they have an equivalent in the ES5 specification, and they are: `each`, `map`, and `reduce`.

Underscore each

In the first example, we used the ES5 function `Array.prototype.forEach` to iterate the initial dataset. Underscore also provides its own version called `_.each()`. The main difference from the `Array.prototype.forEach` function is that `_.each()` can be used against object properties if an object rather than array is provided as its first argument. The full function signature is `_.each(list, iteratee, [context])` and it will call the second function parameter `iteratee` against each item of the iterated `list` object or array passed as its first argument. To use this function in the second example `starter-example-with-underscore.find` from this chapter, we just need to replace this line from the `getBicyclesCountPerType()` function:

```
bicycles.forEach(function(bicycle) {
```

With line:

```
_.each(bicycles, function(bicycle) {
```

Underscore `each` has a `forEach` alias, so it can be called in a similar way with its ES5 equivalent:

```
_.forEach(bicycles, function(bicycle) {
```

Another difference from the ES5 equivalent is that Underscore `each` returns the first parameter as opposed to `undefined` allowing further function call chaining. Underscore also has first class support for function chaining that will be detailed in *Chapter 4, Programming Paradigms with Underscore.js*.

We will explore calling `each` over object properties together with other Underscore functions mentioned in this chapter in *Chapter 2, Using Underscore.js with Collections*.

Underscore map and reduce

The next Underscore functions of special interest are `map` and `reduce`. The Underscore `map` function signature is similar to the `each` function signature: `_.map(list, iteratee, [context])`. It transforms a `list` array or object parameter into a new array that contains modified elements or property values of the `list` parameter. The transformation is made by:

- Iterating the elements or properties of the `list` parameter using the second parameter function `iterate`, and calling this function for each item;
- Collecting the values of the `iteratee` call into the array returned by the `_.map()` function.

Underscore `reduce` is a function that converts an array or object properties into a single value. The function signature is `_.reduce(list, iteratee, [memo], [context])` and the optional `memo` parameter is used as the seed for the returned value. If `memo` is not specified, then the first element or object property value of the `list` parameter will be used as the seed value instead. The `iteratee` function signature is `iteratee(memo, element, index, list)` when `list` is an array like object. The value returned by `iteratee` is either supplied as the `memo` parameter for the next iteration or is returned as the final `reduce` value if there are no more iterations left.

The next example will showcase these two functions by iterating over an array of people that have received an important award at some point in their lives — the Nobel prize for literature. The example calculates the age when the award was received using `_.map()` and the average value of the age when the award was received using `_.reduce()`.

This is the initial dataset:

```
var people = [{
    name: "Herta Muller",
    birthYear: 1953,
    awardYear: 2009
}, {
    name: "Mario Vargas Llosa",
    birthYear: 1936,
    awardYear: 2010
}, {
    name: "Tomas Transtromer",
    birthYear: 1931,
    awardYear: 2011
}, {
    name: "Mo Yan",
    birthYear: 1955,
    awardYear: 2012
}, {
    name: "Alice Munro",
    birthYear: 1931,
    awardYear: 2013
}, {
    name: "Patrick Modiano",
    birthYear: 1945,
    awardYear: 2014
}];
```

First, we calculate the age when the award was received for each person by using
`_.map()`:

```
var peopleWithAwardAge = _.map(people, function(person){
  return {
    name: person.name,
    awardAge: person.awardYear - person.birthYear
  }
});
```

Next, we calculate the average age of the award by using `_.reduce()` and passing `0`
as the `memo` seed value:

```
var totalAge = _.reduce(peopleWithAwardAge, function(memo, person) {
  return memo + person.awardAge;
}, 0);
var averageAwardAge = totalAge / peopleWithAwardAge.length;
```

You can explore the complete example in the `underscore.map.reduce` folder from
the source code for this chapter or by running it directly at `http://bit.ly/1MMSOlc`.

Functional programming fundamentals

In the previous example, we transformed an existing dataset into a new structure
rather than modifying it (mutating it) by using the two powerful Underscore functions
`_.map()` and `_.reduce()`. This is a typical example of a functional programming style
in action: we use functions also known as higher-order functions that accept other
functions as parameters, and we don't alter (mutate) the state of variables such as
`people` and `peopleWithAwardAge` once they are created — the data that we work
with is immutable.

Functional programming (FP) is a declarative programming paradigm in which
functions are first class citizens that are treated as values (data), and the application
code avoids mutating existing states. In an FP language, you also find that:

- Functions called **higher-order functions** can be used to compose other
  functions by accepting functions as arguments or by returning functions.

- Functions that don't have side effects are called **pure functions**, and if they
  are called repeatedly with the same parameters, they return the same result.
  They don't have any dependency on data outside their function scope.

There are many aspects of FP such as extensive use of recursion, employing lazy evaluation, and built-in support for pattern matching that are implemented to various degrees in FP languages. Languages such as Erlang, Haskell, Clojure, and F# (to name just a few) are considered functional languages, while languages such as C#, JavaScript, and Java 8 have limited support for a functional programming style. Languages such as Scala are classified as object-functional — a bridge between FP and OOP (object-oriented programming) paradigms.

JavaScript can be used in a functional programming style through its built in support for functions as first class citizens, higher-order functions, by simulating immutability and using its limited recursion capabilities. We will explore JavaScript functional aspects in *Chapter 4, Programming Paradigms with Underscore.js* and where needed in other chapters.

Useful patterns and practices for JavaScript applications targeting ECMAScript 5

The examples we have used so far had an introductory role and they are not representative of a production ready application. One of the goals of this book is to present examples that are closer to real life usage and the rest of the examples will follow this goal. As a first step, we need to introduce some JavaScript patterns and practices that will be useful in organizing and driving the rest of the examples in this book. They are essential when writing ES5 code, but you don't need them when writing ES6 code using classes and modules (more details about ES6 and how it improves code quality will be discussed in *Chapter 6, Related Underscore.js Libraries and ECMAScript Standards*).

One of the difficult problems to solve when writing JavaScript code is to avoid the pollution of the global scope. Any variable declared outside of a function body will automatically be visible in the global scope. You can easily imagine a scenario where your variable names clash with the variables defined in other JavaScript files or libraries. Also, JavaScript automatically moves all variable declarations to the top of the current scope. This behavior is called **hoisting** and can lead to scenarios where you use a variable before it is declared, which is confusing and can cause unintended errors.

To avoid these problems, a typical workaround is to use a function body to declare your variables. Variables declared in this way belong to the local scope of the enclosing function, and they are invisible to the global scope. This workaround is based on two patterns used frequently in JavaScript applications: the **immediately invoked function expression** (IIFE) — pronounced "iffy" — and the **revealing module pattern**.

The immediately-invoked function expression

If we append the line, `console.log(people.length);`, at the end of the `script` section from the previous example found in the `underscore.map.reduce` folder, we will see the length of the array written in the console as **6**. If we convert the example to use an immediately invoked function expression, the `script` section will look like the following code (with most of the code removed for brevity):

```
(function(){
  var people = [...];
  $(document).ready(function() {...});
}());
console.log(people.length);
```

You can view the preceding example either online at `http://bit.ly/1WNL31t` or in the `underscore.map.reduce-iife` folder from the source code for this chapter.

I have highlighted the changes required to convert the code to use the immediately invoked function expression. Sometimes, a leading semicolon is used to prevent issues caused by the automatic semicolon insertions in JavaScript when your scripts get concatenated with other scripts. The enclosing parentheses around the highlighted self-executing anonymous function and before the last semicolon are the signature for these types of expression.

The example will still work as before, but the console output will have this message: `Uncaught ReferenceError: people is not defined`. Using this pattern, we made the `people` variable inaccessible for the global scope, while leaving it available for the IIFE function scope. The Underscore library is using an IIFE that contains all its source code and we will follow suit by ensuring the rest of the examples will use this pattern whenever applicable.

Next, we will explore a JavaScript pattern that also prevents exposing data to the global scope and is useful for safely sharing application code between different components in JavaScript.

The revealing module pattern

The revealing module pattern solves the problem of hiding implementation details for JavaScript objects that expose property-like objects or functions to the global scope. The following example is a plain JavaScript one — no external library references are required:

```html
<!DOCTYPE html>
<html>
<head>
  <meta charset="utf-8" />
  <title>Getting started - Revealing module pattern</title>
</head>
<body>
  <h1>See browser console for example output.</h1>
  <script>
    var revealingModule = (function() {
      var innerObject = 5;
      var innerFunction = function(value) {
        return innerObject + value;
      };
      return {
        outerObject1: innerFunction(1),
        outerObject2: innerFunction(2),
        outerFunction: innerFunction
      };
    }());
    console.log("outerObject1:" + revealingModule.outerObject1);
    console.log("outerObject2:" + revealingModule.outerObject2);
    console.log("innerObject:" + revealingModule.innerObject);
    console.log("outerFunction(3):" +
    revealingModule.outerFunction(3));
    console.log("innerFunction(3):" +
    revealingModule.innerFunction(3));
  </script>
</body>
</html>
```

You can view the example either online at `http://bit.ly/1hUg2J5` or in the `revealing-module-pattern` folder from the source code for this chapter.

The first highlighted code represents the object created through the revealing module pattern, and you will notice that it relies on an IIFE to define itself. Using this pattern, all of the variables declared inside the IIFE are inaccessible to the outside scope, and the only visible properties are the ones returned in the object created in the last highlighted code snippet. The console output for this example is shown as follows:

```
outerObject1:6

outerObject2:7

innerObject:undefined

outerFunction(3):8

Uncaught TypeError: undefined is not a function
```

Any reference to the variables defined within the IIFE will be unsuccessful as demonstrated by the exception raised when the `innerFunction` was called within the global scope. You will see this pattern in action throughout this book, as we will use it in many examples. The Underscore library is using a version of this pattern and exposes all its global accessible functions though its _ object. The annotated Underscore source code available at `http://underscorejs.org/docs/underscore.html` is great for exploring how the library works behind the covers and is the recommended companion for this book.

 You can find more information about the revealing module pattern and other JavaScript design patterns in the online resource *Learning JavaScript Design Patterns, Addy Osmani, O'Reilly Media,* available at `http://addyosmani.com/resources/essentialjsdesignpatterns/book/`.

Next, we will convert the `underscore.map.reduce-iife` example code to use the revealing module pattern and define a global accessible object called `awardAgeCalculator`. This object exposes all relevant functions that need to be accessible outside the IIFE scope as shown in the next code snippet:

```
var awardAgeCalculator = (function() {
  var getPeople = function() {
    return [{
      name: "Herta Muller",
      birthYear: 1953,
      awardYear: 2009
    }, {
      ...
    }, {
      name: "Patrick Modiano",
      birthYear: 1945,
```

```
        awardYear: 2014
    }];
};

var innerGetPeopleWithAwardAge = function() {
    return _.map(getPeople(), function(person) {
        return {
            name: person.name,
            awardAge: person.awardYear - person.birthYear
        };
    });
};

return {
    getPeopleWithAwardAge: innerGetPeopleWithAwardAge,
    getAverageAwardAge: function() {
        var peopleWithAwardAge = innerGetPeopleWithAwardAge();
        var totalAwardAge = _.reduce(peopleWithAwardAge,
        function(memo, person) {
            return memo + person.awardAge;
        }, 0);
        return totalAwardAge / peopleWithAwardAge.length;
    }
};
}());
```

You can find the example in the `underscore.map.reduce-revealing-module` folder from the source code for this chapter or you can execute it online at `http://bit.ly/1h7eg6x`.

I have highlighted the two functions that are defined in the local IIFE scope and cannot be accessed directly unless they are referenced as properties in the object returned by the `awardAgeCalculator` IIFE. Notice the functional style used in the example; apart from the `awardAgeCalculator` object, we use only functions throughout and don't have any variable inside `awardAgeCalculator` that preserves its value between any two function calls. We will continue to use this approach to define the core functionality of an example and here is how `awardAgeCalculator` is used to generate the example output as part of the same example:

```
$(document).ready(function() {
    var outputContent = "<br />Award age for people:";
    _.each(awardAgeCalculator.getPeopleWithAwardAge(),
    function(person) {
```

```
      outputContent += "<br />";
      outputContent += " - " + person.name + " was " +
      person.awardAge + " years old";
   });
   var averageAwardAge =
   Math.floor(awardAgeCalculator.getAverageAwardAge());
   outputContent += "<br /><br />" + "Average award age is " +
   averageAwardAge + " years old.";
   $("#output").html(outputContent);
});
```

I have highlighted the usages of the awardAgeCalculator functions, and we obtained a better separation of the code and simplified the example output section.

We can encounter an issue if we reference other JavaScript files that might also declare an awardAgeCalculator variable. Choosing the name of your global accessible objects is very important because of this issue, and it is a very difficult problem to solve without a dependency management utility. We will discuss how we can avoid this issue and other ways to organize JavaScript code in *Chapter 6, Related Underscore.js Libraries and ECMAScript Standards*.

The JavaScript strict mode

ES5 has introduced a new way to use a stricter variant of JavaScript called **strict mode**. This variant changes the behavior of the JavaScript runtime, and the following are some changes that occur in strict mode:

- Some silent errors are thrown instead of being ignored, such as assignment to a nonwritable property.

- All global variables need to be explicitly declared. When you mistype a global variable name, an exception is thrown.

- All of the property names of an object need to be unique, and all of the parameter names for a function also need to be unique.

By including the line "use strict"; in your scripts, you can adhere to this JavaScript variant when using a modern ES5-compliant browser. If the script is loaded in an older browser, the statement is ignored and the JavaScript is parsed in non-strict mode. Strict mode can only be safely declared at the top of a function body. If it is declared in the global scope, it can cause issues when a strict mode script is concatenated with other non-strict scripts.

Using strict mode leads to safer, cleaner code with fewer errors. All examples throughout the rest of the book will use the patterns and practices discussed in this section.

Setting up a development workflow for exploring Underscore

The examples we used so far can be executed directly and their external JavaScript dependencies such as jQuery and Underscore are referenced using publicly hosted files. This is great for quick examples and rapid prototyping but not a recommended practice when building any non-trivial application. We will next set up a development workflow that is popular with JavaScript developers. This workflow will help us build examples efficiently and is close to what a real-life JavaScript application will use.

Modern JavaScript development with Node.js

The process of building modern JavaScript applications is greatly simplified by leveraging the rich ecosystem powered by Node.js.

Node.js is a software runtime for building server-side applications using JavaScript. Internally, it uses the V8 JavaScript engine that powers the Google Chrome web browser to compile JavaScript code to native code before executing it. It is based on an asynchronous event-driven programming model with non-blocking I/O operations using a single thread of execution. This makes it a great fit for real-time applications and high-throughput web applications. Node.js benefits from all the optimizations and performance improvements that Google Chrome has introduced since its first version and it runs on all major operating systems: Linux, Mac OS X, and Windows.

The Node.js installation comes with a built-in package manager called npm that contains a very large number of packages. There is an online npm packages repository available at `https://www.npmjs.org/` that is used for installing or updating Node.js application dependencies.

For setting up the Node.js environment, we will target the Windows operating system first with Mac OS X and Linux covered next.

Windows

You need to install Node.js, which comes in 32-bit and 64-bit versions by going to `https://nodejs.org/download/`, and select one of the packages that matches your OS. You can use `https://nodejs.org/dist/v0.12.7/node-v0.12.7-x86.msi` for the 32-bit version or `https://nodejs.org/dist/v0.12.7/x64/node-v0.12.7-x64.msi` for the 64-bit version (the available versions may be different at the time you are reading this book). We have used the 64-bit version with the examples from this book. As an alternative installation method, you can use the Chocolatey package manager for Windows and install it using the instructions provided at `https://chocolatey.org` or by executing the following line in a Command Prompt with administrator privileges (opened using the **Run as administrator** option):

```
@powershell -NoProfile -ExecutionPolicy Bypass -Command "iex ((new-object
net.webclient).DownloadString('https://chocolatey.org/install.ps1'))" &&
SET PATH=%PATH%;%ALLUSERSPROFILE%\chocolatey\bin
```

With Chocolatey now available, we can use it to install Node.js by executing the following command:

```
choco install -y node.js
```

Mac OS X

On Mac OS X, we will use the Homebrew package manager for OS X that can be installed by following the instructions at `http://brew.sh` or by executing the following command line in the terminal:

```
ruby -e "$(curl -fsSL https://raw.githubusercontent.com/Homebrew/install/
master/install)"
```

With Homebrew now available, we can use it to install Node.js by executing the following command:

```
brew install node
```

Linux

Ubuntu 14.04 was the target Linux distribution used to test the examples from this book, but you should be able to use any Linux distribution you prefer. Ubuntu comes with its built-in package manager, and we will use it to execute the commands requires to register the Node.js repository used in this book (more details at `http://bit.ly/1hcVaMm`):

```
sudo apt-get install -y curl
```

```
curl -sL https://deb.nodesource.com/setup_0.12 | sudo bash -
```

With the Node.js repository now configured in Ubuntu, we can install Node.js with the following command:

```
sudo apt-get install -y nodejs
```

Verifying Node.js installation

To verify that Node.js has installed correctly, we need to open the OS-specific Command Prompt and execute the following command:

```
node -v
```

If you see v0.12.07 on the screen, it means that Node.js has installed correctly, and we can execute all the examples from this book without any other OS-level changes.

 We will explore more about Node.js and npm packages in *Chapter 5, Using Underscore.js in the Browser, on the Server, and with the Database*.

Managing JavaScript dependencies with Bower

With Node.js installed, we have access to its large repository of development tools and libraries provided through npm. We will use npm to install Bower, which is a package manager optimized for web sites and web applications. Bower is very similar to npm with the main difference being that Bower packages maintain a flat dependency tree as opposed to npm packages that maintain a deep nested dependency tree. For example, if two Bower packages have a dependency on Underscore, only one version of the Underscore package will be installed. If two npm packages have a dependency on Underscore, each package will install its Underscore package separately (although npm 3 will use flat dependencies by default similar to Bower).

 Bower has a dependency on the Git source control system, which can be installed from this location http://git-scm.com/downloads.

To install Bower, you need to open a Command Prompt and execute this npm command:

```
npm install -g bower
```

Notice the -g npm command-line switch, which installs the package in the machine specific npm packages folder. By default, npm packages are installed relative to the current directory unless this command switch is specified. From now on, Bower will be available to all our examples regardless of the folder in which they reside.

Next, we will use the previous example found in the underscore.map.reduce-revealing-module folder from the source code for this chapter and transform it into a new example that leverages Bower for package management.

By running the following command in the example folder, we will create a bower.json file that holds metadata about the current project and its dependencies:

```
bower init
```

When running this command, there are a series of Command Prompt options that can be accepted with their default values. The values will be updated in the bower.json file. Next, we will install the Bower packages that match the required JavaScript library dependencies for jQuery and Underscore:

```
bower install jquery#2.1.4 --save
bower install underscore#1.8.3 --save
```

Notice the package name jquery followed by the version target #2.1.4 that ensures that we are using only a specific version of a Bower package rather than the latest version available when we omit the version target. The last command-line switch --save will persist the package information in the bower.json file allowing an easy restore for the Bower packages if they get deleted locally or they are not committed with the source code for the current project.

We now have the two JavaScript libraries installed in the current folder within a bower_components subfolder, which is the default Bower location for storing packages.

We can now change the JavaScript references in the index.html file to point to the two local Bower packages rather than the online hosted files:

```
<script src="bower_components/jquery/dist/jquery.js"></script>
<script src="bower_components/underscore/underscore.js"></script>
```

I have also moved the inline JavaScript code into two separate files called awardAgeCalculator.js and index.js that separate the core functionality in the former from the output specific code in the latter. You can find the example in the underscore.map.reduce-with-local-dependencies folder from the source code for this chapter.

By leveraging Bower, we can quickly reference any JavaScript library that is needed while making it very easy to share the current project with other developers or even publish it to the Bower package repository.

Choosing a JavaScript editor

We are approaching the end of the first chapter, and so far, we have not mentioned any tool for editing the code used in the example. Actually, we don't really have to as modern JavaScript development relies on a command-line-based tool chain usually based on Node.js. The workflow we established for exploring the examples from this book does not require a specific visual editor to be installed. You could just use the default operating system text editor and stop at that. However, it is worth mentioning the existing rich ecosystem of JavaScript visual editors and IDEs that is available if you want to benefit from additional functionality.

There are both commercial and free to use tools available, and they are separated into two categories: tools that have a main focus on Node.js and JavaScript-based development, and tools for general development that support Node.js and JavaScript through a plugin system. Note that we mentioned both Node.js and JavaScript as requirements for any editor or IDE as Node.js will be used extensively later on in this book.

Out of the Node.js and JavaScript-specific commercial tools, it is worth mentioning WebStorm IDE (more details at `https://www.jetbrains.com/webstorm/`) and Cloud9 online IDE that allows browser-based JavaScript development among other languages (more details at `https://c9.io/`). There is even a free Microsoft Visual Studio plugin called Node.js Tools for Visual Studio development (more details at `http://nodejstools.codeplex.com/`).

Out of the editors supporting JavaScript via their plugin system, I will mention the commercial editor Sublime Text (free trial available, more details at `http://www.sublimetext.com/`) and the free and open editor Atom (`https://atom.io/`). Atom itself was built using Node.js, has a rich plugin ecosystem, and is the editor used to author all the code from this book. To install Atom, you can follow the instructions available at `http://bit.ly/1EiGYwn`.

Of course there are many other tools available out there, but these are the ones that I personally found useful for learning how to build JavaScript applications.

You can execute all the examples from this book without having to install or configure anything just by using Cloud9 IDE (free registration required) at the project address `https://ide.c9.io/alexpop/underscorejs-examples`.

Testing JavaScript code with Jasmine

Maintaining complex JavaScript codebases is challenging due to the dynamic nature of the language and the lack of built-in module support (up until ES6). Applying unit testing practices helps alleviate these issues and JavaScript as a language benefits from a large number of unit testing frameworks, libraries, and tools.

We will now add tests for the previous example found in the `underscore.map.reduce-with-local-dependencies` folder from the source code for this chapter. To implement these tests we will use Jasmine, a popular test framework.

Jasmine is a **behavior-driven development (BDD)** framework that contains extensive built-in functionality to define and execute tests for JavaScript code. A BDD framework differs from other test frameworks such as QUnit by defining tests as a desired behavior, where the test outcome is specified first followed by the actual test assertion. Jasmine uses a `describe/it` syntax to define test specifications, while other BDD frameworks use a `given/when/then` syntax. Using BDD tests produces output similar to a specification document and these types of tests are usually called **specs**. Other advantages of using Jasmine are that it does not rely on any other library, it has a rich functionality for defining tests and tests assertions, and it has great documentation available at `http://jasmine.github.io`.

Jasmine introduction

A typical Jasmine test that asserts the result of a trivial JavaScript operation will have the following code (with the Jasmine specific functions highlighted):

```
describe("A basic JavaScript add operation", function() {
  it("should be correct", function() {
    var result = 1 + 1;
    expect(result).toEqual(2);
  });
});
```

When running the test, its output should read **A basic JavaScript add operation should be correct**, forming a meaningful statement about the value delivered by the code being tested. The `describe` call is a Jasmine global function that will group one or more test specifications that are defined by the `it` function (which is also another Jasmine global function). Both functions have a test-related description as the first argument. The second argument is a function that defines the test suite in its body with the test specification (or the spec) defined in the `it` function. Test assertions use the Jasmine global function `expect`, which is chained with a helper function called **matcher** that will facilitate the test result evaluation.

There are a couple of built-in matcher functions available, such as `toBe()`, which checks whether the test assertion object and the expected object are the same; `toEqual()`, which checks whether the two objects are equivalent; and `toBeDefined()`, which checks whether the test assertion object is not `undefined`. You can also define your own custom matchers for more complex expectation checks. Jasmine allows you to set up and tear down data before and after a spec is executed through the global functions `beforeEach()` and `afterEach()`.

Adding tests using the default Jasmine infrastructure

Before creating the tests, we need to modify the `awardAgeCalculator.js` file that contains the code under test (or **SUT — system under test**) and ensure it is testable. A SUT is testable if it allows swapping out its dependencies, if it can be tested in isolation and does not depend on a shared or global application state.

For our example, we need to test that the two global accessible (or public) functions of the `awardAgeCalculator` object (the SUT) are producing the expected results when executed against specific data sets. Currently, we cannot easily swap out the default array of people used in the example and we need to change it by making the `getPeople()` function public and changing the rest of the functions to accept an input array as highlighted in the next code snippet:

```
var awardAgeCalculator = (function() {
  "use strict";

  var getPeople = function() {
    return [{
      name: "Herta Muller",
      birthYear: 1953,
      awardYear: 2009
    }, {
      ...
    }, {
      name: "Patrick Modiano",
      birthYear: 1945,
      awardYear: 2014
    }];
  };

  return {
    getPeople: getPeople,
```

```
      calculateAwardAgeForPeople: function(people) {
        return _.map(people, function(person) {
          return {
            name: person.name,
            awardAge: person.awardYear - person.birthYear
          };
        });
      },
      getAverageAwardAgeForPeople: function(people) {
        var peopleWithAwardAge =
        this.calculateAwardAgeForPeople(people);
        return _.reduce(peopleWithAwardAge, function(memo, person) {
          return memo + person.awardAge;
        }, 0) / peopleWithAwardAge.length;
      }
    };
}());
```

We also exposed the getPeople() function to the global scope for convenient access to the default data set. By making these changes, we have created a testable SUT where we can alter the input data for the two functions we plan to test. We can now write the tests by creating a spec\awardAgeCalculatorSpec.js file and using the following code:

```
describe("Given awardAgeCalculator", function() {
  describe(
    "when calling calculateAwardAgeForPeople()",
    function() {
      var people;
      var peopleWithAwardAge;
      beforeEach(function() {
        people = awardAgeCalculator.getPeople();
        peopleWithAwardAge =
        awardAgeCalculator.calculateAwardAgeForPeople(people);
      });
      it(
        "then the award age for the first person should be
        correct",
        function() {
          expect(peopleWithAwardAge[0].name).toEqual("Herta
          Muller");
          expect(peopleWithAwardAge[0].awardAge).toEqual(56);
        });
      it(
```

```
                "then the award age of the last person should be correct",
                function() {
                  expect(peopleWithAwardAge[peopleWithAwardAge.length -
                  1].name).toEqual("Patrick Modiano");
                  expect(peopleWithAwardAge[peopleWithAwardAge.length -
                  1].awardAge).toEqual(69);
                });
            });
        describe(
          "when calling getAverageAwardAgeForPeople()",
          function() {
            var people;
            var aveargeAwardAge;
            beforeEach(function() {
              people = awardAgeCalculator.getPeople();
              aveargeAwardAge =
              awardAgeCalculator.getAverageAwardAgeForPeople(people);
            });
            it("then the average award age should be correct",
            function() {
              expect(Math.floor(aveargeAwardAge)).toEqual(69);
            });
          });
    });
```

The tests are defined within two nested `describe` functions and we used a
`beforeEach` function to avoid code duplication when exercising the SUT. The
expectations for the first set of tests are verifying that the person name and the
award age are correct.

To execute these tests, we need to add Jasmine support to our example. We will
use Bower to install Jasmine as a development package (a package that can be
omitted when the current project is deployed to a target environment) through
the following command:

```
bower install jasmine#2.3.4 --save-dev
```

We will change the default `SpecRunner.html` file provided with the standalone
Jasmine distribution at `http://bit.ly/1EhdgHT` to reference the files from the
Bower package together with the SUT file (the code file) and the test file
as highlighted in the following code:

```
<!DOCTYPE HTML>
<html>
<head>
```

```html
    <meta http-equiv="Content-Type" content="text/html; charset=UTF-
8">
    <title>Jasmine Spec Runner v2.3.4</title>
    <link rel="shortcut icon" type="image/png"
href="bower_components/jasmine/images/jasmine_favicon.png">
    <link rel="stylesheet" type="text/css"
href="bower_components/jasmine/lib/jasmine-core/jasmine.css">
    <script type="text/javascript"
src="bower_components/jasmine/lib/jasmine-
core/jasmine.js"></script>
    <script type="text/javascript"
src="bower_components/jasmine/lib/jasmine-core/jasmine-
html.js"></script>
    <script type="text/javascript"
src="bower_components/jasmine/lib/jasmine-
core/boot.js"></script>

    <!-- include source files here... -->
    <script src="bower_components/underscore/underscore.js">
</script>
    <script type="text/javascript" src="awardAgeCalculator.js">
</script>
    <!-- include spec files here... -->
    <script type="text/javascript"
src="spec/awardAgeCalculatorSpec.js"></script>
  </head>
  <body>
  </body>
</html>
```

Notice that we referenced Underscore as a SUT dependency and we don't need any special test output code to display the results other than ensuring that all required JavaScript files are referenced in the SpecRunner.html file. You can find the example in the underscore.map.reduce-with-jasmine folder from the source code for this chapter.

To run the tests, we just need to open the `SpecRunner.html` file in a browser and we should see this output:

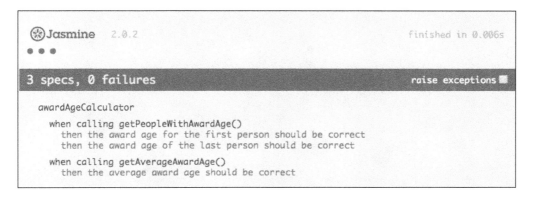

Jasmine tests can also be executed automatically through test runners such as Karma (`http://karma-runner.github.io/`) or Node.js build tools such as Grunt or Gulp. We will discuss these topics in *Chapter 5, Using Underscore.js in the Browser, on the Server, and with the Database* and *Chapter 6, Related Underscore.js Libraries and ECMAScript Standards.*

Summary

This chapter provided an introduction to Underscore and explored useful practices and patterns that will be used throughout the book. We established a development workflow for working efficiently with Underscore examples and we finished the chapter by introducing testing with Jasmine.

Based on these fundamentals, in the next chapter, we will start exploring the Underscore functionality for collections in detail.

Using Underscore.js with Collections

The previous chapter introduced Underscore and presented some of the principles and patterns that will help with using it more efficiently. The chapter concluded by setting up the development workflow used for the book examples.

In this chapter, we will explore Underscore functionality for collections using more in-depth examples. Some of the more advanced concepts related to Underscore functions such as scope resolution and execution context will be explained. The topics of the chapter are as follows:

- Key Underscore functions revisited
- Searching and filtering
- Aggregations and transformations

This chapter assumes that you are familiar with JavaScript fundamentals such as prototypical inheritance and the built-in data types.

The source code for the examples from this chapter is hosted online at `https://github.com/popalexandruvasile/underscorejs-examples/tree/master/collections`, and you can execute the examples using the Cloud9 IDE at the address `https://ide.c9.io/alexpop/underscorejs-examples` from the `collections` folder.

Key Underscore functions revisited – each, map, and reduce

The previous chapter introduced key Underscore functions that are representative of the library and mentioned that some functions can be used with either an array or an object. This flexible approach means that some Underscore functions can operate over **collections**: an Underscore-specific term for arrays, array-like objects, and objects (where the collection represents the object properties). We will refer to the elements within these collections as collection items.

By providing functions that operate over object properties Underscore expands JavaScript reflection like capabilities. Reflection is a programming feature for examining the structure of a computer program, especially during program execution.

JavaScript is a dynamic language without static type system support (as of ES6). This makes it convenient to use a technique called **duck typing** when working with objects that share similar behaviors. Duck typing is a programming technique used in dynamic languages where objects are identified through their structure represented by properties and methods rather than their type (the name of duck typing is derived from the expression "if it walks like a duck, swims like a duck, and quacks like a duck, then it is a duck"). Underscore itself uses duck typing to assert that an object is an array by checking for a property called `length` of type `Number`.

Applying reflection techniques

We will build an example that demonstrates duck typing and reflection techniques through a function that will extract object properties so that they can be persisted to a relational database. Usually a relational database stores objects represented as a data row with column types that map to regular SQL data types.

We will use the `_.each()` function to iterate over object properties and extract those of type `boolean`, `number`, `string`, and `Date` as they can be easily mapped to SQL data types and ignore everything else:

```
var propertyExtractor = (function() {
  "use strict";
  return {
    extractStorableProperties: function(source) {
      var storableProperties = {};
```

```
  if (!source || source.id !== +source.id) {
    return storableProperties;
  }
  _.each(source, function(value, key) {
    var isDate = typeof value === 'object' && value instanceof
    Date;
    if (isDate || typeof value === 'boolean' || typeof value
    === 'number' ||
      typeof value === 'string') {
        storableProperties[key] = value;
      }
  });

  return storableProperties;
    }
  };
}());
```

You can find the example in the `propertyExtractor.js` file within the
`each-with-properties-and-context` folder from the source code for this chapter.

The first highlighted code snippet checks whether the object passed to the
`extractStorableProperties()` function has a property called `id` that is a number.
The `+` sign converts the `id` property into a number and the non-identity operator `!==`
compares the result of this conversion with the unconverted original value. The non-
identity operator returns `true` only if the type of the compared objects is different or
they are of the same type and have different values.

> This was a duck typing technique used by Underscore up until version
> 1.7 to assert whether it deals with an array-like instance or an object
> instance in its collections related functions.
>
> Underscore collection related functions operate over array-like
> objects as they do not strictly check for the built in array object. These
> functions can also work with the `arguments` objects or the HTML
> DOM `NodeList` objects.

The last highlighted code snippet is the `_.each()` function that operates over object
properties using an iteration function that receives the property value as its first
argument and the property name as the optional second argument. If a property has
a `null` or `undefined` value it will not appear in the returned object.

The extractStorableProperties() function will return a new object with all the storable properties. The return value is used in the test specifications to assert that, given a sample object, the function behaves as expected:

```
describe("Given propertyExtractor", function() {
  describe("when calling extractStorableProperties()", function()
  {
    var storableProperties;
    beforeEach(function() {
      var source = {
        id: 2,
        name: "Blue lamp",
        description: null,
        ui: undefined,
        price: 10,
        purchaseDate: new Date(2014, 10, 1),
        isInUse: true,
      };
      storableProperties =
      propertyExtractor.extractStorableProperties(source);
    });
    it("then the property count should be correct", function() {
      expect(Object.keys(storableProperties).length).toEqual(5);
    });
    it("then the 'price' property should be correct", function() {
      expect(storableProperties.price).toEqual(10);
    });
    it("then the 'description' property should not be defined",
    function() {
      expect(storableProperties.description).toEqual(undefined);
    });
  });
});
```

Notice how we used the propertyExtractor global instance to access the function under test, and then we used the ES5 function Object.keys to assert that the number of returned properties had the correct size.

> In a production ready application, we need to ensure that global object names do not clash, among other best practices. We will explore some techniques that will help to achieve this in *Chapter 7, Underscore.js Build Automation and Code Reusability*.

You can find the test specification in the `spec/propertyExtractorSpec.js` file and execute it by browsing the `SpecRunner.html` file from the example source code folder. There is also an `index.html` file that will display the results of the example rendered in the browser using the `index.js` file.

Manipulating the this variable

Many Underscore functions have a similar signature to `_.each(list, iteratee, [context])`, where the optional `context` parameter will be used to set the `this` value for the `iteratee` function when it is called for each collection item. In JavaScript, the built in `this` variable will be different depending on the context where it is used.

We introduced scopes in the previous chapter (*Chapter 1, Getting Started with Underscore.js*), and it is worth mentioning again that using the function scope is the only way to obscure variables' visibility in ES5 JavaScript.

When the `this` variable is used in the global scope context, and in a browser environment, it will return the native `window` object instance. If `this` is used in a function scope, then the variable will have different values:

- If the function is an object method or an object constructor, then `this` will return the current object instance. Here is a short example code for this scenario:

```
var item1 = {
  id: 1,
  name: "Item1",
  getInfo: function(){
    return "Object: " + this.id + "-" + this.name;
  }
};
console.log(item1.getInfo());
// -> "Object: 1-Item1"
```

- If the function does not belong to an object, then `this` will be `undefined` in the JavaScript strict mode. In the non-strict mode, `this` will return its global scope value.

With a library such as Underscore that favors a functional style, we need to ensure that the functions used as parameters are using the `this` variable correctly. Let's assume that you have a function that references `this` (maybe it was used as an object method) and you want to use it with one of the Underscore functions such as `_.each()`. You can still use the function as is and provide the desired `this` value as the `context` parameter value when calling `each`.

I have rewritten the previous example function to showcase the use of the `context` parameter:

```
var propertyExtractor = (function() {
  "use strict";
  return {
    extractStorablePropertiesWithThis: function(source) {
      var storableProperties = {};
      if (!source || source.id !== +source.id) {
        return storableProperties;
      }
      _.each(source, function(value, key) {
        var isDate = typeof value === 'object' && value instanceof
        Date;
        if (isDate || typeof value === 'boolean' || typeof value
        === 'number' ||
          typeof value === 'string') {
            this[key] = value;
          }
      },
      storableProperties);
      return storableProperties;
    }
  };
}());
```

The first highlighted snippet shows the use of `this`, which is typical for an object method. The last highlighted snippet shows the `context` parameter value that `this` was set to. The `storableProperties` value will be passed as `this` for each `iteratee` function call. The test specifications for this example are identical to the previous example, and you can find them in the same folder `each-with-properties-and-context` from the source code for this chapter.

You can use the optional `context` parameter in many of the Underscore functions where applicable and is a useful technique when working with functions that rely on a specific `this` value.

Using map and reduce with object properties

In the previous example, we had some user interface-specific code in
the index.js file that was tasked with displaying the results of the
propertyExtractor. extractStorableProperties() call in the browser.
Let's pull this functionality into another example and imagine that we need a
new function that, given an object, will transform its properties into a format
suitable for displaying in a browser by returning an array of formatted text
for each property. To achieve this, we will use the Underscore _.map()
function over object properties as demonstrated in the next example:

```
var propertyFormatter = (function() {
  "use strict";
  return {
    extractPropertiesForDisplayAsArray: function(source) {
      if (!source || source.id !== +source.id) {
        return [];
      }
      return _.map(source, function(value, key) {
        var isDate = typeof value === 'object' && value instanceof
        Date;
        if (isDate || typeof value === 'boolean' || typeof value
        === 'number' ||
          typeof value === 'string') {
          return "Property: " + key + " of type: " + typeof value
          + " has value: " + value;
        }
        return "Property: " + key + " cannot be displayed.";
      });
    }
  };
}());
```

With Underscore, we can write compact and expressive code that
manipulates these properties with little effort. The test specifications for the
extractPropertiesForDisplayAsArray() function use Jasmine regular
expression matchers to assert the test conditions in the highlighted code
snippets from the following example:

```
describe("Given propertyFormatter", function() {
  describe("when calling extractPropertiesForDisplayAsArray()",
  function() {
```

```
       var propertiesForDisplayAsArray;
       beforeEach(function() {
         var source = {
            id: 2,
            name: "Blue lamp",
            description: null,
            ui: undefined,
            price: 10,
            purchaseDate: new Date(2014, 10, 1),
            isInUse: true,
         };
         propertiesForDisplayAsArray = propertyFormatter.
         extractPropertiesForDisplayAsArray(source);
       });
       it("then the returned property count should be correct",
       function() {
         expect(propertiesForDisplayAsArray.length).toEqual(7);
       });
       it("then the 'price' property should be displayed", function()
       {
         expect(propertiesForDisplayAsArray[4]).toMatch("price.+10");
       });
       it("then the 'description' property should not be displayed",
       function() {
         expect(propertiesForDisplayAsArray[2]).toMatch("cannot be
         displayed");
       });
     });
   });
```

The following example shows how _.reduce() is used to manipulate object properties. This will transform the properties of an object into a format suitable for browser display by returning a string value that contains all the properties in a convenient format:

```
extractPropertiesForDisplayAsString: function(source) {
   if (!source || source.id !== +source.id) {
      return [];
   }
   return _.reduce(source, function(memo, value, key) {
      if (memo && memo !== "") {
         memo += "<br/>";
      }
      var isDate = typeof value === 'object' && value instanceof
      Date;
```

```
        if (isDate || typeof value === 'boolean' || typeof value ===
        'number' ||
          typeof value === 'string') {
          return memo + "Property: " + key + " of type: " + typeof
          value + " has value: " + value;
        }
        return memo + "Property: " + key + " cannot be displayed.";
      },
      "");
}
```

The example is almost identical to the previous one with the exception of the memo accumulator used to build the returned string value.

The test specifications for the extractPropertiesForDisplayAsString() function use a regular expression matcher and can be found in the spec/propertyFormatterSpec.js file:

```
describe("when calling extractPropertiesForDisplayAsString()",
function() {
  var propertiesForDisplayAsString;
  beforeEach(function() {
    var source = {
      id: 2,
      name: "Blue lamp",
      description: null,
      ui: undefined,
      price: 10,
      purchaseDate: new Date(2014, 10, 1),
      isInUse: true,
    };
    propertiesForDisplayAsString =
    propertyFormatter.extractAllPropertiesForDisplay(source);
  });
  it("then the returned string has expected length", function() {
    expect(propertiesForDisplayAsString.length).
    toBeGreaterThan(0);
  });
  it("then the 'price' property should be displayed", function() {
    expect(propertiesForDisplayAsString).toMatch("<br/>Property:
    price of type: number has value: 10<br/>");
  });
});
```

The examples from this subsection can be found within the map.reduce-with-properties folder from the source code for this chapter.

Searching and filtering

In the previous chapter, we used the function `_.find(list, predicate, [context])` to search for a specific item within a collection. This function is part of the Underscore comprehensive functionality for searching and filtering collections represented by object properties and array-like objects. We will make a distinction between `search` and `filter` functions with the former tasked with finding one item in a collection and the latter tasked with retrieving a subset of the collection (although sometimes, you will find the distinction between these functions thin and blurry).

We will revisit the `find` function and the other search-related and filtering-related functions using an example with slightly more diverse data that is suitable for database persistence. We will use the problem domain of a bicycle rental shop and build an array of bicycle objects with the following structure:

```
var getBicycles = function() {
  return [{
    id: 1,
    name: "A fast bike",
    type: "Road Bike",
    quantity: 10,
    rentPrice: 20,
    dateAdded: new Date(2015, 1, 2)
  }, {
  ...
  }, {
    id: 12,
    name: "A clown bike",
    type: "Children Bike",
    quantity: 2,
    rentPrice: 12,
    dateAdded: new Date(2014, 11, 1)
  }];
};
```

Each bicycle object has an `id` property, and we will use the `propertyFormatter` object built in the previous section to display the example's results in the browser for your convenience.

The code was shortened here for brevity (you can find its full version alongside the other examples from this section within the `searching` and `filtering` folders from the source code for this chapter). All the examples are covered by tests and these are the recommended starting points if you want to explore them in detail.

Searching

For the first example in this section, we will define a bicycle-related requirement where we need to search for a bicycle of a specific type and with a rental price under a maximum value. Compared to the previous _.find() example, we will start with writing the test's specifications first for the functionality that is yet to be implemented. This is a test-driven development approach where we will define the acceptance criteria for the function under test first followed by the actual implementation. Writing the tests first forces us to think about what the code should do, rather than how it should do it, and this helps eliminate waste by writing only the code required to make the tests pass.

Underscore find

The test specifications for our initial requirement are as follows:

```
describe("Given bicycleFinder", function() {
  describe("when calling findBicycle()", function() {
    var bicycle;
    beforeEach(function() {
      bicycle = bicycleFinder.findBicycle("Urban Bike", 16);
    });
    it("then it should return an object", function() {
      expect(bicycle).toBeDefined();
    });
    it("then the 'type' property should be correct", function() {
      expect(bicycle.type).toEqual("Urban Bike");
    });
    it("then the 'rentPrice' property should be correct",
    function() {
      expect(bicycle.rentPrice).toEqual(15);
    });
  });
});
```

The highlighted function call `bicyleFinder.findBicycle()` should return one bicycle object of the expected type and price as asserted by the tests.

 It is important to note that in all the book tests, we are not checking whether the Underscore functions are working correctly. We only test the application code to ensure our expectations about the application functionality are correct.

Here is the implementation that satisfies the test specifications:

```
var bicycleFinder = (function() {
  "use strict";
  var getBicycles = function() {
    return [{
      id: 1,
      name: "A fast bike",
      type: "Road Bike",
      quantity: 10,
      rentPrice: 20,
      dateAdded: new Date(2015, 1, 2)
    }, {
      ...
    }, {
      id: 12,
      name: "A clown bike",
      type: "Children Bike",
      quantity: 2,
      rentPrice: 12,
      dateAdded: new Date(2014, 11, 1)
    }];
  };
  return {
    findBicycle: function(type, maxRentPrice) {
      var bicycles = getBicycles();
      return _.find(bicycles, function(bicycle) {
        return bicycle.type === type && bicycle.rentPrice <=
        maxRentPrice;
      });
    }
  };
}());
```

The code returns the first bicycle that satisfies the search criteria ignoring the rest of the bicycles that might meet the same criteria.

You can browse the index.html file from the searching folder within the source code for this chapter to see the result of calling the bicyleFinder.findBicycle() function displayed on the browser via the propertyFormatter object.

Underscore some

There is a closely related function to `_.find()` with the signature `_.some(list, [predicate], [context])`. This function will return `true` if at least one item of the `list` collection satisfies the `predicate` function. The `predicate` parameter is optional, and if it is not specified, the `_.some()` function will return `true` if at least one item of the collection is not `null`. This makes the function a good candidate for implementing guard clauses. A guard clause is a function that ensures that a variable (usually a parameter) satisfies a specific condition before it is used any further. The next example shows how `_.some()` is used to perform checks that are typical for a guard clause:

```
var list1 = [];
var list2 = [null, , undefined, {}];
var object1 = {};
var object2 = {
  property1: null,
  property3: true
};
if (!_.some(list1) && !_.some(object1)) {
  alert("Collections list1 and object1 are not valid when calling
  _.some() over them.");
}
if(_.some(list2) && _.some(object2)){
  alert("Collections list2 and object2 have at least one valid
  item and they are valid when calling _.some() over them.");
}
```

If you execute this code in a browser, you will see both alerts being displayed. The first alert gets triggered when an empty array or an object without any properties defined are found. The second alert appears when we have an array with at least one element that is not `null` and is not `undefined` or when we have an object that has at least one property that evaluates as `true`.

Going back to our bicycle data, we will define a new requirement to showcase the use of `_.some()` in this context. We will implement a function that will ensure that we can find at least one bicycle of a specific type and with a maximum rental price.

The code is very similar to the `bicycleFinder.findBicycle()` implementation with the difference that the new function returns `true` if the specific bicycle is found (rather than the actual object):

```
hasBicycle: function(type, maxRentPrice) {
  var bicycles = getBicycles();
  return _.some(bicycles, function(bicycle) {
    return bicycle.type === type && bicycle.rentPrice <=
    maxRentPrice;
  });
}
```

You can find the test specifications for this function in the `spec/bicycleFinderSpec.js` file from the `searching` example folder.

Underscore findWhere

Another function similar to `_.find()` has the signature `_.findWhere(list, properties)`. This compares the property key-value pairs of each collection item from `list` with the property key-value pairs found on the `properties` object parameter. Usually, the `properties` parameter is an object literal that contains a subset of the properties of a collection item. The `_.findWhere()` function is useful when we need to extract a collection item matching an exact value compared to `_.find()` that can extract a collection item that matches a range of values or more complex criteria.

To showcase the function, we will implement a requirement that needs to search a bicycle that has a specific `id` value. This is how the test specifications look:

```
describe("when calling findBicycleById()", function() {
  var bicycle;
  beforeEach(function() {
    bicycle = bicycleFinder.findBicycleById(6);
  });
  it("then it should return an object", function() {
    expect(bicycle).toBeDefined();
  });
  it("then the 'id' property should be correct", function() {
    expect(bicycle.id).toEqual(6);
  });
});
```

And the next code snippet from the `bicycleFinder.js` file contains the actual implementation:

```
findBicycleById: function(id){
  var bicycles = getBicycles();
  return _.findWhere(bicycles, {id: id});
}
```

Underscore contains

In a similar vein to the `_.some()` function, there is a `_.contains(list, value)` function that will return `true` if there is at least one item from the `list` collection that is equal to the `value` parameter. The equality check is based on the strict comparison operator `===` where the operands will be checked for both type and value equality.

We will implement a function that checks whether a bicycle with a specific `id` value exists in our collection:

```
hasBicycleWithId: function(id) {
  var bicycles = getBicycles();
  var bicycleIds = _.pluck(bicycles,"id");
  return _.contains(bicycleIds, id);
}
```

Notice how the `_.pluck(list, propertyName)` function was used to create an array that stores the `id` property value for each collection item. In its implementation, `_.pluck()` is actually using `_.map()`, acting like a shortcut function for it.

Filtering

As we mentioned at the beginning of this section, Underscore provides powerful filtering functions, which are usually tasked with working on a subsection of a collection. We will reuse the same example data as before, and we will build some new functions to explore this functionality.

Underscore filter

We will start by defining a new requirement for our data where we need to build a function that retrieves all bicycles of a specific type and with a maximum rental price.

This is how the test specification looks for the yet to be implemented function `bicycleFinder.filterBicycles(type, maxRentPrice)`:

```
describe("when calling filterBicycles()", function() {
  var bicycles;

  beforeEach(function() {
    bicycles = bicycleFinder.filterBicycles("Urban Bike", 16);
  });

  it("then it should return two objects", function() {
    expect(bicycles).toBeDefined();
    expect(bicycles.length).toEqual(2);
  });

  it("then the 'type' property should be correct", function() {
    expect(bicycles[0].type).toEqual("Urban Bike");
    expect(bicycles[1].type).toEqual("Urban Bike");
  });

  it("then the 'rentPrice' property should be correct", function()
  {
    expect(bicycles[0].rentPrice).toEqual(15);
    expect(bicycles[1].rentPrice).toEqual(14);
  });
});
```

The test expectations are assuming the function under test `filterBicycles()` returns an array, and they are asserting against each element of this array.

To implement the new function, we will use the `_.filter(list, predicate, [context])` function that returns an array with all the items from the `list` collection that satisfy the `predicate` function. Here is our example implementation code:

```
filterBicycles: function(type, maxRentPrice) {
  var bicycles = getBicycles();
  return _.filter(bicycles, function(bicycle) {
    return bicycle.type === type && bicycle.rentPrice <=
    maxRentPrice;
  });
}
```

The usage of the _.filter() function is very similar to the _.find() function with the only difference in the return type of these functions.

You can find this example together with the rest of the examples from this subsection within the filtering folder from the source code for this chapter.

Underscore where

Underscore defines a shortcut function for _.filter() which is _.where(list, properties). This function is similar to the _.findWhere() function, and it uses the properties object parameter to compare and retrieve all the items from the list collection with matching properties.

To showcase the function, we defined a new requirement for our example data where we need to retrieve all bicycles of a specific type. This is the code that implements the requirement:

```
filterBicyclesByType: function(type) {
  var bicycles = getBicycles();
  return _.where(bicycles, {
    type: type
  });
}
```

By using _.where(), we are in fact using a more compact and expressive version of _.filter() in scenarios where we need to perform exact value matches.

Underscore reject and partition

Underscore provides a useful function, which is the opposite of _.filter() and has a similar signature: _.reject(list, predicate, [context]). Calling the function will return an array of values from the list collection that do not satisfy the predicate function. To show its usage, we will implement a function that retrieves all bicycles with a rental price less than or equal to a given value. Here's the function implementation:

```
getAllBicyclesForSetRentPrice: function(setRentPrice) {
  var bicycles = getBicycles();
  return _.reject(bicycles, function(bicycle) {
    return bicycle.rentPrice > setRentPrice;
  });
}
```

Using the _.filter() function alongside the _.reject() function with the same list collection and predicate function will allow us to partition the collection into two arrays. One array holds items that do satisfy the predicate function, while the other holds items that do not satisfy the predicate function.

Underscore has a more convenient function that achieves the same result, and this is _.partition(list, predicate). It returns an array that has two array elements—the first has the values that would be returned by calling _.filter() using the same input parameters and the second has the values for calling _.reject().

Underscore every

We mentioned _.some() as being a great function for implementing guard clauses. It is also worth mentioning another closely related function _.every(list, [predicate], [context]). The function will check every item of the list collection and will return true if every item satisfies the predicate function or if list is null, undefined or empty. If the predicate function is not specified, the value of each item will be evaluated instead. If we use the same data from the guard clause example for _.some(), we will get the opposite results, as shown in the next example:

```
var list1 = [];
var list2 = [null, , undefined, {}];
var object1 = {};
var object2 = {
  property1: null,
  property3: true
};
if (_.every(list1) && _.every(object1)) {
  alert("Collections list1 and object1 are valid when calling
  _.every() over them.");
}
if(!_.every(list2) && !_.every(object2)){
  alert("Collections list2 and object2 do not have all items valid
  so they are not valid when calling _.every() over them.");
}
```

To ensure a collection is not null, undefined, or empty and each item is also not null or undefined, we should use both _.some() and _.every() as part of the same check, as shown in the following example:

```
var list1 = [{}];
var object1 = { property1: {}};
```

```
if (_.every(list1) && _.every(object1) && _.some(list1) &&
_.some(object1)) {
  alert("Collections list1 and object1 are valid when calling both
  _some() and _.every() over them.");
}
```

If the `list1` object is an empty array or an object without properties, when we call `_.every(list1)` we get the result `true`. When we call `_.some(list1)` for an empty array or an object without properties we get the result `false`. Hence we can use both functions to validate a collection and ensure it has at least one element or one object property.

These code examples demonstrate how you can build your own guard clauses or data validation rules by using simple Underscore functions. We will explore more data validation topics in *Chapter 4, Programming Paradigms with Underscore.js*.

Aggregations and transformations

We dealt so far with functions tasked with extracting a value or a range of values from collections, and we will now move to functions that aggregate or transform collections. Aggregate functions operate over an entire collection to extract or calculate a single value or a limited set of values. Transformation functions operate over an entire collection and return a new collection that is usually a different representation of the original collection.

The first example of an aggregate function was `_.reduce()` and the first example of a transformation function was `_.map()`. The former calculates an accumulator value from the entire collection and the latter creates a new collection from the original collection.

Aggregations

We will use our example data for this chapter to revisit `_.reduce()` and define a new requirement to calculate the average rental price for all bicycles or for bicycles of a specific type. We will implement the `getAverageRentalPrice(type)` function that will return the average rental price for all bicycles when the `type` parameter is not specified. First of all, we will define the tests for this new function in the `spec/bicycleAggregatorSpec.js` file:

```
describe("Given bicycleAggregator", function() {
  describe("when calling getAverageRentalPrice()", function() {
```

```
        var averageRentalPrice =
        bicycleAggregator.getAverageRentalPrice();
        it("then it should be correct", function() {
          expect(averageRentalPrice).toBeCloseTo(16.83);
        });
      });
      describe("when calling getAverageRentalPrice() for urban
      bicycles", function() {
        var averageRentalPrice =
        bicycleAggregator.getAverageRentalPrice("Urban Bike");
        it("then it should be correct", function() {
          expect(averageRentalPrice).toBeCloseTo(15.33);
        });
      });
    });
```

The tests assume the function is implemented in a global `bicycleAggregator` object similar to the `bicycleFinder` object from the previous sections. Notice we highlighted the Jasmine matcher function `toBeCloseTo()`, which allows us to approximate the expected value down to the desired precision.

The `getAverageRentalPrice(type)` function implementation should be familiar as we already used a similar example in *Chapter 1, Getting Started with Underscore.js*:

```
getAverageRentalPrice: function(type) {
  var bicycles = getBicycles();
  var filteredBicycles = bicycles;
  if (type) {
    filteredBicycles = _.where(bicycles, {
      type: type
    });
  }
  return _.reduce(filteredBicycles, function(memo, bicycle) {
    return memo + bicycle.rentPrice;
  }, 0) / _.size(filteredBicycles);
}
```

First, we extracted a subset of the collection using the `_.where()` function if the `type` parameter is specified (if the `type` parameter is not specified, we will operate on the entire collection created by the `getBicycles` call). Then, we accumulated all the rental prices using `_.reduce()` and we divided the final value with the size of the collection.

Notice that instead of using `filteredBicycles.length` to get the collection size, we used the `_.size()` function that also works with plain objects not only with array-like objects. If we pass a plain object to the `_.size()` function, we can get back the number of properties, and if we pass an array-like object, we get back the length of the array.

You can find this example together with the other examples from this subsection in the `aggregations` folder from the source code for this chapter. For convenience, the `index.html` file can be opened in the browser to view the example's output.

Underscore max and min

Underscore provides two specialized aggregate functions: `_.max(list, [iteratee], [context])` and `_.min (list, [iteratee], [context])`, which work with collections. The second optional parameter `iteratee` is a function called for each collection item and its return value is used for comparison. If `iteratee` is not specified, then the value of the collection item itself will be used for comparison.

To apply these functions to our example data, we will define two new requirements. The first one is to create a function that will return the most recently added bicycle for a given bicycle type. If the bicycle type is not specified, the function should return the most recently added bicycle across all bicycle types. To satisfy this requirement, we will implement a new function with the signature `getMostRecentlyAddedBicycle(type)`.

The previous example for the `getAverageRentalPrice(type)` function had a section where we retrieved the bicycles for a given `type` parameter:

```
var bicycles = getBicycles();
var filteredBicycles = bicycles;
if (type) {
  filteredBicycles = _.where(bicycles, {
    type: type
  });
}
```

As we need the same code in our new function, we will move it into its own function:

```
var filterBicyclesByType = function(bicycles, type) {
  if (!type) {
    return bicycles;
  }
  return _.where(bicycles, {
    type: type
  });
};
```

Next, we will use the `filterBicyclesByType()` and `_.max()` functions to extract the bicycle with the most recent added date:

```
getMostRecentlyAddedBicycle: function(type) {
  var filteredBicycles = filterBicyclesByType(getBicycles(),
  type);
  return _.max(filteredBicycles, function(bicycle) {
    return bicycle.dateAdded;
  });
}
```

The highlighted `iteratee` function extracts the bicycle added date for comparison and can be easily changed to calculate a different value used for comparison.

For the second requirement of our example data, we need a function that will return the lowest priced bicycle for a given bicycle type. If the bicycle type is not specified, the function should return the lowest priced bicycle across all bicycle types. In implementing the requirement, we will use the `_.min()` function and its usage should be familiar from the previous example:

```
getLowestPricedBicycle: function(type) {
  var filteredBicycles = filterBicyclesByType(getBicycles(),
  type);
  return _.min(filteredBicycles, function(bicycle) {
    return bicycle.rentPrice;
  });
}
```

The test specifications for the `getLowestPricedBicycle` function ensures that the returned bicycle is not `null` or `undefined` by using the Jasmine `toBeTruthy()` matcher and it also checks that the returned bicycle has the expected `id` value:

```
describe("when calling getLowestPricedBicycle() for urban
bicycles", function() {
  var bicycle = bicycleAggregator.getLowestPricedBicycle("Urban
  Bike");
  it("then it should be correct", function() {
    expect(bicycle).toBeTruthy();
    expect(bicycle.id).toEqual(8);
  });
});
```

Transformations

We have already seen the _.map() function used in some of the previous examples. In itself, this function represents one of the most simple and powerful transformations, and we will use it alongside another useful transformation function in the following example.

Underscore sortBy

We will define a new requirement for our sample data where we need to extract an array of bicycles ordered by their rental price. The array should contain strings that have the bicycle information formatted for display and should be optionally filtered by the bicycle type.

In implementing this requirement, we will use _.map() alongside _.sortBy(list, iteratee, [context]). The latter function will sort a collection by a specific property name (passed as the iteratee string value) or by using a calculated value (returned by iteratee when it is passed as a function).

For the examples within this section, we have defined a bicycleTransformer object that implements the current requirement in the getBicyclesSortedByRentPrice() function:

```
getBicyclesSortedByRentPrice: function(type) {
  var filteredBicycles = filterBicyclesByType(getBicycles(),
  type);
  var sortedBicycles = _.sortBy(filteredBicycles, 'rentPrice');
  return _.map(sortedBicycles, function(bicycle) {
    return bicycle.name + " - " + bicycle.type + " : " +
    bicycle.rentPrice;
  });
}
```

We created a sorted array of bicycle objects first, and then we extracted a formatted string from every bicycle returned in a final array. We tested the returned array object as well as some of its elements in the spec/bicycleTransformerSpec.js file:

```
describe("when calling getBicyclesSortedByRentPrice()", function()
{
  var sortedBicycles =
  bicycleTransformer.getBicyclesSortedByRentPrice();
  it("then it returns an array of correct length", function() {
    expect(sortedBicycles).toBeTruthy();
    expect(sortedBicycles.length).toEqual(12);
```

```
  });
  it("then the first bicycle should be correct", function() {
    expect(sortedBicycles[0]).toEqual("A blue bike - Children Bike
    : 10");
  });
  it("then the last bicycle should be correct", function() {
    expect(sortedBicycles[sortedBicycles.length - 1]).toEqual("An
    all-terain bike - Mountain Bike : 27");
  });
});
```

You can find all the examples from this subsection within the `transformations` folder from the source code for this chapter. For convenience, the `index.html` file can be opened in the browser to view the example's output.

Underscore groupBy

Another useful transformation is grouping objects based on a specific criteria. Underscore provides a `_.groupBy(list, iteratee, [context])` function that groups collection items into arrays. The arrays representing the groups are stored as properties of the object returned by this function. The property names of the returned objects are also the distinct values that represent a group. The group values are either returned by calling the `iteratee` function or are property values of the collection items when `iteratee` is provided as a string.

Our example implements a function that groups bicycles by their added year (the bicycles are optionally filtered by the bicycle type):

```
getBicyclesGroupedByYear: function(type) {
  var filteredBicycles = filterBicyclesByType(getBicycles(),
  type);

  return _.groupBy(filteredBicycles, function(bicycle) {
    return bicycle.dateAdded.getFullYear();
  });
}
```

We used the `iteratee` function to calculate the added year from the bicycle `dateAdded` property and the year value appears as a property name on the result object. In the test specifications, the result object's properties are accessed using the bracket notation (because they are numbers, they cannot be accessed using the dot notation as with valid property names):

```
describe("when calling getBicyclesGroupedByYear()", function() {
  var groupedBicycles =
  bicycleTransformer.getBicyclesGroupedByYear();
```

```
it("then it returns an object with two properties", function() {
  expect(groupedBicycles).toBeTruthy();
  expect(_.size(groupedBicycles)).toEqual(2);
});
it("then the bicycle count for year 2014 should be correct",
function() {
  expect(groupedBicycles['2014'].length).toEqual(8);
});
it("then the bicycle count for year 2015 should be correct",
function() {
  expect(groupedBicycles['2015'].length).toEqual(4);
});
});
```

For the next example, the `iteratee` parameter is provided as a string, and we implement a function that groups bicycles by their rental price values:

```
getBicyclesGroupedByPrice: function(type) {
  var filteredBicycles = filterBicyclesByType(getBicycles(),
  type);

  return _.groupBy(filteredBicycles, 'rentPrice');
}
```

Similar to the previous example, the result object's properties cannot be accessed through the dot notation as they are numbers so the bracket notation is used instead within its test specifications:

```
describe("when calling getBicyclesGroupedByPrice()", function() {
  var groupedBicycles =
  bicycleTransformer.getBicyclesGroupedByPrice();
  it("then it returns an object with 10 properties", function() {
    expect(groupedBicycles).toBeTruthy();
    expect(_.size(groupedBicycles)).toEqual(10);
  });
  it("then the bicycle count for lowest price should be correct",
  function() {
    expect(groupedBicycles['10'].length).toEqual(2);
  });
  it("then the bicycle count for highest price should be correct",
  function() {
    expect(groupedBicycles['27'].length).toEqual(1);
  });
});
```

Underscore indexBy

Our example data revolves around an array of bicycle objects and each time we need to find a specific bicycle, we have to process each array item until it is found. If the array is considerably bigger and we have to repeatedly search for bicycles, we will end up with an implementation that might be lacking in efficiency and performance.

Underscore provides a function that converts a collection to an object with properties mapped to each collection item. The property name is either a unique property value or a unique calculated value of the collection item. The Underscore function that provides this functionality is `_.indexBy(list, iteratee, [context])` and the `iteratee` parameter can be a string value representing a property name of a collection item or a function that returns a unique value for a collection item. The object returned by `_.index()` allows us to find a collection item very quickly without having to iterate through the collection as exemplified next.

For the code example, we will implement a function that returns an object where all property names are values of the bicycle `id` property so that we can retrieve any bicycle using its `id` value:

```
getBicyclesIndexedById: function() {
  var bicycles = getBicycles();
  return _.indexBy(bicycles, 'id');
}
```

We used the `_.indexBy` function with the `iteratee` parameter supplied as a string, but we could replace it with an alternative implementation where `iteratee` is passed as a function:

```
getBicyclesIndexedById: function() {
  var bicycles = getBicycles();
  return _.indexBy(bicycles, function(bicycle){ return
  bicycle.id;});
}
```

The test specifications provide an example of how the return object can be used to access a bicycle for which we know its `id` value:

```
describe("when calling getBicyclesIndexedById()", function() {
  var indexedBicycles =
  bicycleTransformer.getBicyclesIndexedById();
  it("then it returns an object with 12 properties", function() {
    expect(indexedBicycles).toBeTruthy();
    expect(_.size(indexedBicycles)).toEqual(12);
  });
```

```
it("then the first indexed bicycle should be correct",
function() {
  expect(indexedBicycles['1'].name).toEqual('A fast bike');
});
it("then the last indexed bicycle count should be correct",
function() {
  expect(indexedBicycles['12'].name).toEqual('A clown bike');
});
});
```

Underscore countBy

We already used _.countBy in *Chapter 1, Getting Started with Underscore.js*, but now we can understand it better in the context of transformation functions. The function _.countBy(list, iteratee, [context]) is very similar to _.groupBy() as it groups collection items based on a group key with the difference that it stores the group count rather than the actual group in the return object properties.

We will use an example suitable for our bicycle data sample and define a new requirement to extract an object that contains the bicycle count for each bicycle type. The code that implements the new getBicyclesCountByType() function is succinct:

```
getBicyclesCountByType: function() {
  var bicycles = getBicycles();
  return _.countBy(bicycles, 'type');
}
```

The iteratee parameter is a string in our example, but it can be also supplied as a function (see *Chapter 1, Getting Started with Underscore.js*, for the starter example).

The test specifications show how the object returned by the getBicyclesCountByType() function is accessed:

```
describe("when calling getBicyclesCountByType()", function() {
  var bicyclesCount = bicycleTransformer.getBicyclesCountByType();
  it("then it returns an object with 4 properties", function() {
    expect(bicyclesCount).toBeTruthy();
    expect(_.size(bicyclesCount)).toEqual(4);
  });
  it("then the bicycle count for 'Urban Bike' should be correct",
  function() {
    expect(bicyclesCount['Urban Bike']).toEqual(3);
  });
```

```
  it("then the bicycle count for 'Road Bike' should be correct",
  function() {
    expect(bicyclesCount['Road Bike']).toEqual(2);
  });
});
```

Other collection-based functions

There are three more collection transformation functions that we will mention briefly here:

- `_.toArray(list)` creates a native `Array` object from a collection.
- `_.shuffle(list)` creates an array of randomized collection items using the **Fisher-Yates shuffle** algorithm.
- `_.sample(list, [n])` also creates an array of randomized collection items with an optional limit of *n* array items. If *n* is not specific, it returns one random item from the collection.

The last collection specific function for this chapter is `_.invoke(list, methodName, *arguments)` that will call method `methodName` for each collection item and will optionally pass an arguments list to the invoked method.

Summary

In this chapter, we explored many of the collection specific functions as provided by Underscore. We revisited some of the functions introduced in the previous chapter and demonstrated additional functionality. We continued with searching and filtering functions and finished with aggregation and transformation functions.

In the next chapter, we will demonstrate the Underscore features covering arrays, functions, and objects.

3
Using Underscore.js with Arrays, Objects, and Functions

The previous chapter explored the functionality provided by Underscore.js for collections. This chapter will continue in the same vein and will further explore the specialized features that Underscore implements for:

- Arrays
- Objects
- Functions
- Utility functions

The chapter assumes that you are familiar with the JavaScript built-in data types.

The source code for the examples from this chapter is hosted online at `https://github.com/popalexandruvasile/underscorejs-examples/tree/master/arrays-objects-functions`, and you can execute the examples using Cloud9 IDE at the address `https://ide.c9.io/alexpop/underscorejs-examples` from the `arrays-functions-objects` folder.

Arrays

The Underscore functions targeting collections worked with array-like objects or object properties. In this section, we will look into more specific functions that work with the `Array` object or with array-like objects such as the `arguments` variable that is available in any JavaScript function body.

First, we will expand the sample data we used in the previous chapter by adding an array of client objects for our bicycle rental universe. Each client has rented at least one bicycle and has a `registered` date property and a `preferredBike` property holding the name of an existing bicycle. The client object has other standard properties such as `name`, `gender`, and `email`. We can use a website such as `www.json-generator.com` to define and randomly generate the required JSON data in a larger quantity that is suitable for more involved examples. A sample of such a client object is as follows:

```
{
  "id": 4,
  "name": "Virgie Glenn",
  "gender": "female",
  "company": "SPHERIX",
  "email": "virgieglenn@spherix.com",
  "phone": "+1 (931) 540-3924",
  "address": "810 Dikeman Street, Aberdeen, Nevada, 9711",
  "registered": "2014-03-03T04:45:09 -00:00",
  "preferredBike": "An all-terain bike",
  "bikePoints": 3342,
  "isActive": true,
  "notes": "Sit do fugiat esse consequat commodo incididunt ex.
  Et exercitation elit commodo enim exercitation consectetur culpa
  officia est excepteur officia proident officia. Ex adipisicing
  dolore pariatur cupidatat labore. Consequat labore laboris
  dolore eiusmod sint laborum veniam do cillum ut culpa eiusmod.
  In dolore adipisicing ea consectetur incididunt enim magna nulla
  sint do dolore mollit. Cillum dolor velit consectetur aute.\r\n"
}
```

The template file `clients.json.template` was used to generate the sample data and can be found in the source code for this chapter within the `arrays` folder. We also have a `dataProvider.js` file that contains the previous `getBicycles()` function that returns the bicycle sample data, together with a new function `getClients()` that returns the client sample data used in this chapter (and which was generated using the `clients.json.template` file).

Extracting array start and end sequences

Underscore provides four useful functions that facilitate working with array elements located at the beginning or the end:

- `_.first(array, [n])` extracts the first n elements from `array`. If n is not specified, it returns the first element of the array.

- `_.rest(array, [index])` is the complement of the `_.first` function and extracts `array` elements starting from the `index` position. If `index` is not specified, it extracts all `array` elements except the first element.

- `_.last(array, [n])` extracts the last n elements from `array`. If n is not specified, it returns the last element of `array`.

- `_.initial(array, [n])` is the complement of the `_.last` function and extracts all `array` elements except the last n elements. If n is not specified, it extracts all `array` elements except the last element.

For our sample data, we will define two complementary requirements to showcase the first two functions `_.first` and `_.rest`. The first gives us a list of the oldest clients so that they can be given a special discount; the second gives us a list of all other clients so that we can give them a normal discount. We will create a new `clientRetriever` object that contains two functions: `getOldestClients(count)`, which retrieves the oldest clients for a special discount; and `getNewerClients(skipFirstCount)`, which retrieves the rest of the clients, who will get a normal discount.

We will first write the test specifications for two new functions in the `spec/clientRetrieverSpec.js` file:

```
describe("when calling getOldestClients()", function() {
  var clients = clientRetriever.getOldestClients(5);
  it("then it returns an array of correct length", function() {
    expect(clients).toBeTruthy();
    expect(clients.length).toEqual(5);
  });
  it("then the first client should be correct", function() {
    expect(clients[0]).toBeTruthy();
    expect(clients[0].id).toEqual(150);
  });
  it("then the last client should be correct", function() {
    expect(clients[clients.length - 1]).toBeTruthy();
    expect(clients[clients.length - 1].id).toEqual(243);
  });
});
describe("when calling getNewerClients()", function() {
  var clients = clientRetriever.getNewerClients(5);
  it("then it returns an array of correct length", function() {
    expect(clients).toBeTruthy();
    expect(clients.length).toEqual(245);
  });
});
```

```
it("then the first client should be correct", function() {
  expect(clients[0]).toBeTruthy();
  expect(clients[0].id).toEqual(85);
});
it("then the last client should be correct", function() {
  expect(clients[clients.length - 1]).toBeTruthy();
  expect(clients[clients.length - 1].id).toEqual(69);
});
});
```

The test specifications are ensuring the assumptions about our data sample are correct when using the functions under test and they are not meant to test the Underscore functionality. They are also useful for showing how the functions under test are actually called. This is the implementation of our new functions from the clientRetriever.js file, and the following code can be read side by side with the test specifications for a richer context:

```
var clientRetriever = (function() {
  "use strict";
  var clients = dataProvider.getClients();
  return {
    getOldestClients: function(count) {
      return _.first(_.sortBy(clients, function(client) {
        return new Date(client.registered);
      }), count);
    },
    getNewerClients: function(skipFirstCount) {
      return _.rest(_.sortBy(clients, function(client) {
        return new Date(client.registered);
      }), skipFirstCount);
    }
  };
}());
```

By calling _.sortBy(), we ensured the array is sorted by the registered property value before extracting the required sequence. Notice how we combined two Underscore functions in the same line of code, which is representative for a functional programming style that we will explore more in *Chapter 4, Programming Paradigms with Underscore.js*.

For the _.last() and _.initial() functions, we will define two other complementary requirements: to get a list of the newest clients so that we can send them a survey about the ease of use of the client registration process; and to get a list of all the other clients so that we can send them an overall satisfaction survey. The implementation of the two new functions getNewestClients(count) and getOlderClients(skipLastCount) is as follows:

```
getNewestClients: function(count) {
  return _.last(_.sortBy(clients, function(client) {
    return new Date(client.registered);
  }), count);
},
getOlderClients: function(skipLastCount) {
  return _.initial(_.sortBy(clients, function(client) {
    return new Date(client.registered);
  }), skipLastCount);
}
```

You can view the test specifications in the spec/clientRetrieverSpec.js file and the examples rendered output by browsing to the index.html file.

We have used concise and expressive Underscore functions to manipulate the start and end of an array with little effort. The functions presented in this chapter are more powerful as they are narrower in their scope compared with the functions presented in *Chapter 2, Using Underscore.js with Collections*.

 The four functions explored in this subsection use Array. prototype.slice to implement their functionality. You could use this function directly, but I found the Underscore functions easier to understand and closer to natural language.

Union, intersect, and related functions

Underscore provides a series of useful functions for working with multiple arrays. The first one is _.union(*arrays) where the *arrays notation represents one or more array objects passed as parameters. This function returns an array with unique elements collected from the input arrays. The elements are collected in the order they appear in the input arrays from left to right, and any element that is already collected is ignored. The unique elements are verified using the strict equality operator ===.

For its associated example, we will define a new sample data requirement to get the combination of the oldest and best clients in order to give them a special discount by e-mail. By "best clients" we mean the ones who have the highest values in the bikePoints property (which stores the accumulated value of a client's bicycle rentals since they first registered). The combination should have unique clients to avoid sending duplicate e-mails. We will define a new function clientRetriever. getOldestOrBestClients() with the following test specifications:

```
describe("when calling getOldestOrBestClients()", function() {
  var clients = clientRetriever.getOldestOrBestClients(50);
  it("then it returns an array of correct length", function() {
    expect(clients).toBeTruthy();
    expect(clients.length).toEqual(89);
  });
});
```

Some of the code for the function being tested should be familiar as it was used in the previous subsection:

```
getOldestOrBestClients: function(count) {
  var oldestClients = _.first(_.sortBy(clients, function(client) {
    return new Date(client.registered);
  }),
  count);
  var bestClients = _.last(_.sortBy(clients, 'bikePoints'),
  count);
  var oldestOrBestClients = _.union(oldestClients, bestClients);
  return oldestOrBestClients;
}
```

We have created two separate arrays: one with the clients sorted by the registered property value, the other with clients sorted by the bikePoints property value; and we have used _.union() to return the array of unique clients that are present in any of the input arrays. The client objects are compared by reference and they are guaranteed to be unique as they were all created as part of the dataProvider. getClients() call.

 If you need more information about reference comparisons and the strict equality operator, I recommend an insightful article on the **Mozilla Developer Network (MDN)** website at http://mzl.la/1O4fFWk.

An alternative way to implement `getOldestOrBestClients()` is through the use of the `_.uniq(array, [isSorted], [iteratee])` function. This function will return only unique elements from the `array` parameter and these unique elements were compared using the strict equality operator `===`. The optional `iteratee` parameter function provides a custom identifier value if required and the optional `isSorted` parameter should be set to `true` if `array` is already sorted for an improvement in performance. Here is the alternative implementation using `_.uniq()`:

```
getOldestOrBestClientsWithuniq: function(count) {
  var oldestClients = _.first(_.sortBy(clients, function(client) {
      return new Date(client.registered);
    }),
    count);
  var bestClients = _.last(_.sortBy(clients, 'bikePoints'),
  count);
  var oldestOrBestClientsWithDuplicates =
  oldestClients.concat(bestClients);
  return _.uniq(oldestOrBestClientsWithDuplicates);
}
```

The first two lines are identical to the previous function `getOldestOrBestClients()` and we used `Array.prototype.concat()` to create a single array that is processed further by the `_.uniq()` function. The test specifications for the new `getOldestOrBestClientsWithuniq()` function are identical to the ones for the `getOldestOrBestClients()` function as they achieve the same functionality.

We will now look at multiple intersecting arrays and define a new requirement for our sample data to get both the oldest and best clients so that we can send them a bigger discount code via e-mail. We will use the `_.intersection(*arrays)` function that works on multiple arrays and extracts the unique elements that appear in all input arrays. Here is the implementation for the `getOldestOrBestClients()` function that fulfills the new requirement:

```
getOldestAndBestClients: function(count) {
  var oldestClients = _.first(_.sortBy(clients, function(client) {
      return new Date(client.registered);
    }),
    count);
  var bestClients = _.last(_.sortBy(clients, 'bikePoints'),
  count);
  var oldestAndBestClients = _.intersection(oldestClients,
  bestClients);
  return oldestAndBestClients;
}
```

Again, the first two lines are identical to the `getOldestOrBestClients()` function, but if you look at the test specifications, you will notice that we expect a result of 11 clients from the top 50 best and top 50 oldest clients. This is considerably smaller compared to the 89 clients expected for the same input data in the test specifications for the `getOldestOrBestClients()` function.

We have the functionality provided by `getOldestOrBestClients()` to send a discount to all our best or oldest clients, but we need to make sure we exclude the ones returned by `getOldestAndBestClients()`, as they will receive a different (and better) discount. Underscore help us with this requirement through the `_.difference(array, *others)` function that returns only elements from the `array` parameter that are not present in any of the arrays provided through the `others` parameters. Here is the code that will extract the difference between the two sets of clients:

```
getOldestOrBestClientsThatAreNotBoth: function(count) {
  var oldestClients = _.first(_.sortBy(clients, function(client) {
      return new Date(client.registered);
    }),
    count);
  var bestClients = _.last(_.sortBy(clients, 'bikePoints'),
  count);
  var oldestOrBestClients = _.union(oldestClients, bestClients);
  var oldestAndBestClients = _.intersection(oldestClients,
  bestClients);
  return _.difference(oldestOrBestClients, oldestAndBestClients);
}
```

The test specifications for the `getOldestOrBestClientsThatAreNotBoth()` function expects a result of 78 clients that ties in with the previous test specifications expectations.

Alongside the `_.difference()` function, there is a `_.without(array, *values)` function that will remove one or more elements provided as additional parameters (represented by the `*values` notation) from the `array` parameter.

Other array-related functions

Underscore also provides the functionality for transposing arrays through the `_.zip(*arrays)` function. Given one or more arrays as input parameters, it will return an array that contains other arrays as its elements. Each array element contains the elements from all input arrays located at the current index, as demonstrated in the following code snippet:

```
var array1 = [0,1,2,4];
```

```
var array2 = ['a', 'b', 'c'];
var array3 = [{ id: 1}, {id:2}];
var zippedArray = _.zip(array1, array2, array3);
console.log(zippedArray);
// -> [[0, "a", { id: 1 }],
//     [1, "b", { id: 2 }],
//     [2, "c", undefined],
//     [4, undefined, undefined]]
```

To use _.zip() with our bicycle-related examples, we will introduce a new data sample that contains the client orders as represented by the object from the next example (generated using a similar JSON template as the one used for clients):

```
{
  "clientId": 2,
  "orders": [{
    "bicycleName": "A modern bike",
    "quantity": 4
  }, {
    "bicycleName": "An all-terrain bike",
    "quantity": 1
  }]
}
```

The function dataProvider.getClientOrders() returns an array of client orders that matches the indexes of the clients returned in dataProvider.getClients().

We will define a new requirement to extract an array of elements that are also arrays that contain client data and order count, so it can be processed further. The code that implements this requirement can be found in the clientRetriever.js file:

```
getClientsAndOrdersAsArrays: function() {
  var clientIds = _.pluck(clients, 'id');
  var clientNames = _.pluck(clients, 'name');

  var clientOrders = dataProvider.getClientOrders();
  var ordersCount = _.map(clientOrders, function(clientOrder) {
    return clientOrder.orders.length;
  });

  var clientAndOrders = _.zip(clientIds, clientNames,
  ordersCount);
  return clientAndOrders;
}
```

We extracted three distinct arrays initially: one with the client `id` properties, one with the client `name` properties and last one with the order count for each client. We then applied `_.zip()` for these three arrays and the result is an array that contains 250 arrays (one array for each client). Each array within the result array contains three elements: the client `id` value, the client `name` value, and the client order count value.

You can browse the `index.html` file to see the output for the `getClientsAndOrdersAsArrays()` function or look at the `spec/clientRetrieverSpec.js` file to see its test specifications. They can be found in the `arrays` folder from the source code for this chapter.

We will mention the remaining array-related functions briefly:

- `_.unzip(*arrays)`: This has the reverse effect `_.zip()`, as demonstrated in the following code snippet:

```
var unzippedArray = _.unzip(
  [[0, "a", { id: 1 }],
   [1, "b", { id: 2 }],
   [2, "c", undefined],
   [4, undefined, undefined]]);
console.log(unzippedArray);
// -> [[0, 1, 2, 4],
//     ["a", "b", "c", undefined],
//     [{ id: 1 }, { id: 2 }, undefined, undefined]]
```

- `_.compact(array)`: This eliminates any element that is either `null`, `undefined`, `false`, `0`, `""`, or `NaN`, which is useful for cleaning up arrays of undesired values.

- `_.flatten(array, [shallow])`: This checks every element of the `array` parameter, and if it is an array itself, it will pull its elements into the returned array alongside the other non-array elements. Unless `shallow` is set to `true`, the function will operate on more than one level and will pull any array elements into the top-level array regardless of their nesting depth.

- `_.object(list, [values])`: This creates an object that has properties with keys specified in the `list` array parameter and values specified in the `values` array parameter. If the `values` parameter is not specified, then the `list` parameter should be an array of arrays that contain a key and value pair.

- `_.indexOf(array, value, [isSorted])`: This returns the index at which the `value` parameter can be found as an element of the `array` parameter. If `value` cannot be found, then the return value is -1. For large arrays that are known to be sorted, you can pass `isSorted` as `true` for a faster binary search.

- `_.lastIndexOf(array, value, [fromIndex])`: This returns the index at which the last occurrence of the `value` parameter can be found as an element of the `array` parameter. If `value` cannot be found, then the return value is -1. If the `fromIndex` parameter is specified, then the search will start from that index value onwards.

- `_.findIndex(array, predicate, [context])`: This is an alternative to `_.indexOf()` when we need to use a `predicate` function like the one from the `_.find()` function.

- `_.findLastIndex(array, predicate, [context])`: This is an alternative to `_.lastIndexOf()` when we need to use a `predicate` function like the one from the `_.find()` function.

- `_.sortedIndex(list, value, [iteratee], [context])`: This works with a sorted array specified as the `list` parameter. It returns the index at which the `value` parameter needs to be inserted so that the sort order of `list` is maintained. The optional `iteratee` parameter can be a function that is used to calculate the sort order value of an element from the `list` array and of the value parameter, or it can be a property name used to extract the sort order value.

- `_.range([start], stop, [step])`: This generates an array that is a sequence of integer values that starts from 0 or from the `start` parameter (if specified) until the `stop` parameter. The default increment is 1 or `step` when specified.

Objects

Underscore has a series of dedicated functions targeting objects, which extends the features provided for collections.

Underscore keys

We will revisit the `propertyFormatter` related examples to showcase some of the object-related features, and we will start with the function `_.keys(object)`. This function will extract an array containing the names of all enumerable properties from the `object` parameter. It ignores any properties that are inherited, and if you want to include those as well you need to use the `_.allKeys(object)` function instead.

Going back to the original propertyFormatter.
extractPropertiesForDisplayAsArray() function introduced in *Chapter 2, Using Underscore.js with Collections,* we can now change it to use _.keys(object) to ensure we only process objects that have at least one valid property:

```
extractPropertiesForDisplayAsArray: function(source, ignoreId) {
  if (!source || (!ignoreId && source.id !== +source.id) ||
  _.keys(source).length === 0) {
    return [];
  }

  return _.map(source, function(value, key) {
    var isDate = typeof value === 'object' && value instanceof
    Date;
    if (isDate || typeof value === 'boolean' || typeof value ===
    'number' ||
      typeof value === 'string') {
      return "Property: " + key + " of type: " + typeof value + "
      has value: " + value;
    }
    return "Property: " + key + " cannot be displayed.";
  });
}
```

The highlighted code shows the new enhancement and we also added the option of processing objects that don't have an id property that is numeric in line with the propertyFormatter.extractPropertiesForDisplayAsString() function. As a consequence, we can write test specifications for calling the changed function with an empty object represented by {}:

```
describe("when calling extractPropertiesForDisplayAsArray({}, true)
(for an empty object)", function() {
  var propertiesForDisplay;
  beforeEach(function() {
    propertiesForDisplay =
    propertyFormatter.extractPropertiesForDisplayAsArray({},
    true);
  });
  it("then the returned property count should be correct",
  function() {
    expect(propertiesForDisplay.length).toEqual(0);
  });
});
```

You can find the code for all the examples from this section in the `objects` folder from the source code for this chapter.

 The function `_.keys(object)` will use the built in ES5 function `Object.keys()` if available.

Underscore values and pairs

Somewhat similar to `_.keys(object)`, Underscore has `_.values(object)` that extracts an array containing the values of all enumerable properties from the `object` parameter. Another useful function is `_.pairs(object)` that extracts an array of `[key, value]` elements where `key` is a property name and `value` is a property value. We can refactor the `propertyFormatter.extractPropertiesForDisplayAsArray()` function to use `_.pairs()` in combination with `_.each()`:

```
extractPropertiesForDisplayAsArray: function(source, ignoreId) {
  var propertiesForDisplay = [];
  if (!source || (!ignoreId && source.id !== +source.id) ||
  _.keys(source).length === 0) {
    return propertiesForDisplay;
  }
  _.each(_.pairs(source), function(keyValue) {
    var isDate = typeof keyValue[1] === 'object' && keyValue[1]
  instanceof Date;
    if (isDate || typeof keyValue[1] === 'boolean' || typeof
    keyValue[1] === 'number' ||
      typeof keyValue[1] === 'string') {
      propertiesForDisplay.push("Property: " + keyValue[0] + " of
      type: " + typeof keyValue[1] + " has value: " +
      keyValue[1]);
    } else {
      propertiesForDisplay.push("Property: " + keyValue[0] + "
      cannot be displayed.");
    }
  });
  return propertiesForDisplay;
}
```

The highlighted line has replaced the previous version based on _.map() while maintaining the same functionality. If you browse to the SpecRunner.html file, you will receive confirmation that all test specifications are passing even after we made the current changes.

Underscore invert and functions

For more advanced usage scenarios, you can use the _.invert(object) function and switch the object parameter property names with property values, as long as the property values are unique and valid property names.

When using the _.keys() function, you get all properties of an object, including function properties. Underscore provides _.functions(object) that extracts an array that contains the names of all function properties for the object parameter.

To illustrate its usage, we will add a new function propertyFormatter.extractDataPropertiesForDisplayAsArray(source, ignoreId) that returns only properties that are not functions:

```
extractDataPropertiesForDisplayAsArray: function(source, ignoreId) {
  var propertiesForDisplay = [];
  if (!source || (!ignoreId && source.id !== +source.id) ||
  _.keys(source).length === 0) {
    return propertiesForDisplay;
  }
  var functionNames = _.functions(source);
  _.each(_.pairs(source), function(keyValue) {
    var isDate = typeof keyValue[1] === 'object' && keyValue[1]
    instanceof Date;
    if (isDate || typeof keyValue[1] === 'boolean' || typeof
    keyValue[1] === 'number' ||
      typeof keyValue[1] === 'string') {
      propertiesForDisplay.push("Property: " + keyValue[0] + " of
      type: " + typeof keyValue[1] + " has value: " +
      keyValue[1]);
    } else if (!_.contains(functionNames, keyValue[0])) {
      propertiesForDisplay.push("Property: " + keyValue[0] + "
      cannot be displayed.");
    }
  });
  return propertiesForDisplay;
}
```

The highlighted lines will ensure all function properties are ignored, and in the test specifications for this new function, you will notice that we successfully process an object that has a function property besides data properties.

Underscore pick, omit, and has

We already used the _.pluck() function as a convenient shortcut for calling _.map(). There are two functions to extract properties from an object that can be used to build more powerful versions of _.pluck().

The first function is _.pick(object, *keys), where keys can be string values specified as additional parameters or an array of property names and the result is a copy of object that contains only the properties specified in the keys parameter.

The second function is _.omit(object, *keys), where keys can be additional string parameters or an array of property names and the result is a copy of object that contains all its properties except the ones specified in the keys parameter.

In this subsection, we will revisit the bicycle rental sample data and define a new requirement to extract a client array that contains only the id and name properties. The function that implements the new requirement in clientRetriever.js is as follows:

```
getClientsIdAndName: function() {
  return _.map(clients, function(client) {
    return _.pick(client, 'id', 'name');
  });
}
```

The second requirement is to extract only the contact information for all clients, and we will use _.omit() in its implementation:

```
getClientsContactInfo: function() {
  return _.map(clients, function(client) {
    return _.omit(client, 'registered', 'preferredBike',
    'bikePoints', 'isActive', 'notes');
  });
}
```

In both requirements, we created copies of existing client objects, and next we will explore similar functions that enable more advanced object functions.

Underscore extend, clone, and defaults

Underscore provides the `_.extend(destination, *sources)` function that is similar to `jQuery.extend()` and is tasked with copying the properties from one or more source objects into a destination object and returns the modified destination object as a result. If a property with the same name exists in more than one source object, the result property value is taken from the last object where it is present. The function performs a shallow copy—that is, if a destination object has a nested property (an object or an array), it will be copied by reference. In contrast, `jQuery.extend()` supports deep copy, where any nested property that is an object or an array will be copied by calling `jQuery.extend()` in a recursive manner. There is a closely-related function `_.extendOwn(destination, *sources)` that copies properties owned by the source object and ignoring anything that is inherited.

The next function `_.clone(object)` creates a shallow copy for the `object` parameter and in its implementation is actually calling `_.extend({}, object)` to perform the actual copy.

Next, we will discuss the `_.defaults(object, *defaults)` function, where `*defaults` can be one or more additional object parameters. The function will fill in the `object` parameter with properties that belong to any of the `*defaults` object parameters and are `undefined` in the `object` parameter. This means that if a property belongs to more than one `*defaults` object parameters only the value from the first occurrence will be present in the final result.

We will revisit some of these functions in *Chapter 6, Related Underscore.js Libraries and ECMAScript Standards*, where we will explore even more powerful alternatives.

Underscore has, property, propertyOf, and matcher

Underscore has an alternative for the built-in JavaScript function `Object.prototype.hasOwnProperty()` and this is `_.has(object, key)`. Both functions provide the same functionality, with the Underscore function having additional safety in case the built-in JavaScript function has been overwritten.

The following functions facilitate the evaluation of object properties; the first one is `_.property(key)`, which returns a function that will extract the `key` property from an object, as demonstrated in the next example:

```
var item1 = {
```

```
  id: 1,
  name: "Item1"
};
var getName = _.property('name');
console.log(getName(item1));
var item2 = {
  id: 2,
  name: "Item2",
};
console.log(getName(item2));
// -> Item1
//    Item2
```

Its inverse equivalent is _.propertyOf(object), which returns a function that will retrieve a property value from the object parameter as in the following example:

```
var item1 = {
  id: 1,
  name: "Item1"
};
var getItem1 = _.propertyOf(item1);
console.log(getItem1('name'));
var item2 = {
  id: 2,
  name: "Item2",
};
var getItem2 = _.propertyOf(item2);
console.log(getItem2('name'));
// -> Item1
//    Item2
```

The third function is _.matcher(attrs) that returns a predicate function that will check if an object has the property's values specified in the attrs object parameter:

```
var items = [{
  id: 1,
  name: "Item1",
  archived: false
}, {
  id: 2,
  name: "Item2",
  archived: true
}];
```

```
var match = _.matcher({
  archived: true
});
var item = _.find(items, match);
console.log("Found item: " + item.name);
// -> Found item: Item2
```

These functions enable the functional programming paradigm by converting imperative operations, such as getting a property value or comparing multiple property values into functions that can be evaluated later or can be reused by higher-order functions.

Comparing objects and making assertions against objects

As seen so far in this section, Underscore has many useful functions for copying objects, however this presents a problem when we want to compare a copy with the original.

A typical scenario is when we create a copy of an object, pass it to another function, and then persist this copy only if it was modified. Underscore facilitates this scenario through the `_.isEqual(object, other)` function that executes a deep comparison of the two object parameters. The function compares all the property values of the two objects, and if the objects contain nested properties, it will recursively compare them, returning `true` if all property values at any level are equal.

There is another function that can be used in comparisons between objects with signature `_.isMatch(object, properties)` that is closely related to `_.matcher()` (it is actually called by the latter when its return function is invoked). We can say that `_.isMatch()` is the imperative version of `_.matcher()`, as demonstrated in the next example:

```
var items = [{
  id: 1,
  name: "Item1",
  archived: false
}, {
  id: 2,
  name: "Item2",
  archived: true
}];
var foundItem = _.find(items, function(item) {
  return _.isMatch(item, {
```

```
      archived: true
    });
  });
console.log("Found item: " + foundItem.name);
// -> Found item: Item2
```

Underscore has a comprehensive set of functions that can be used to make assertions against objects. These are great when used as predicate functions on their own or in different combinations. We will enumerate them first and then revisit the propertyFormatter.js file and refactor it to use some of these new functions.

These are the assertion functions useful for object validation:

- `_.isEmpty(object)`: This returns `true` if `object` does not have any properties or if the `length` property is 0 when `object` is a string or an array-like object

- `_.isNull(object)`: This returns `true` if the object is `null`

- `_.isUndefined(value)`: This returns `true` if `value` is `undefined`

These are the assertion functions used for determining object types:

- `_.isElement(object)`: This returns `true` if `object` is a Document Object Model (DOM) element

- `_.isArray(object)`: This returns `true` if `object` has the `Array` type

- `_.isObject(value)`: This returns `true` if `object` has the `Object` type, which is applicable to arrays and functions, but not to string and number primitives

- `_.isArguments(object)`: This returns `true` if `object` has the `Arguments` type

- `_.isFunction(object)`: This returns `true` if `object` has the `Function` type; in JavaScript, all functions are of the `Function` type

- `_.isBoolean(object)`: This returns `true` if `object` is strictly equal with `true`, if it is strictly equal with `false`, or has the Boolean type

- `_.isDate(object)`: This returns `true` if `object` has the `Date` type

- `_.isError(object)`: This returns `true` if object inherits from the `Error` object

These are the assertion functions used for `String` objects:

- `_.isString(object)`: This returns `true` if `object` has the `String` type

- `_.isRegExp(object)`: This returns `true` if `object` has the `RegExp` type

And finally, these are the assertion functions used for Number objects:

- _.isNumber(object): This returns true if object has the Number type. This also applies to NaN values.

- _.isFinite(object): This returns true if object has the Number type and is finite.

- _.isNaN(object): This returns true if object has the Number type and is a NaN value. This is the more accurate alternative for the built-in JavaScript isNaN() function that can return true for objects that don't have the Number type.

These functions enable more precise assertions compared with the built-in JavaScript possibilities and introduce an elegant approach to express assertions that is closer to the natural language, making them easier to understand at a glance.

We can now revisit the propertyFormatter.js file and refactor it to use some of the assertions functions and evolve it in a more expressive code base. We will leave the test specifications from the spec/propertyFormatterSpec.js file unchanged and rely on them to ensure that the overall functionality is preserved. All the functions from this file were modified and we will look at extractDataPropertiesForDisplayAsArray implementation as it incorporates most of the changes:

```
extractDataPropertiesForDisplayAsArray: function(source, ignoreId) {
  var propertiesForDisplay = [];
  if (_.isNull(source) || _.isUndefined(source) ||
  _.isEmpty(source) || (!ignoreId && !_.isNumber(source.id))) {
    return propertiesForDisplay;
  }
  _.each(_.pairs(source), function(keyValue) {
    var key = keyValue[0];
    var value = keyValue[1];
    if (_.isDate(value) || _.isBoolean(value) || _.isNumber(value)
|| _.isString(value)) {
      propertiesForDisplay.push("Property '" + key + "' of type: "
      + typeof value + " has value: " + value);
    } else if (!_.isFunction(value)) {
      propertiesForDisplay.push("Property: " + keyValue[0] + "
      cannot be displayed.");
    }
  });
  return propertiesForDisplay;
}
```

We were able to replace the expression that checked whether a property was of the type `Date` with one `_.isDate()` call. We replaced the rather long-winded check whether a property is a function with a single `_.isFunction()` call. A special mention should be made of the code that ensured the `id` property was a number that has now been replaced by a `_.isNumber()` call.

You can find the example for this subsection in the `objects-assertions` folder from the source code for this chapter.

Other object-related functions

Because the function `_.tap(object, interceptor)` is used as part of the chaining functionality of Underscore, we will discuss it in *Chapter 4, Programming Paradigms with Underscore.js*, where wee will also mention the function `_.create(prototype, props)`.

The function `_.mapObject(object, iteratee, [context])` is a version of `_.map()` that only works with objects.

Functions

Underscore has a series of functions that specifically target objects of the type `Function`: it has functions that target other functions. This subsection touches on some of the functional programming concepts that will be explored in detail in *Chapter 4, Programming Paradigms with Underscore.js*.

Functional composition with bind, bindAll, and partial

The first function is `_.bind(function, object, *arguments)` that returns a new function wrapper for the original `function` parameter. The wrapper function has the `this` value set to the `object` parameter and its arguments will be prefilled in order with the values from the `*arguments` parameters. The returned function is also known as **bound** function and is an example of functional composition in action. Through functional composition, we can create new functions based on existing functions in scenarios where we cannot change the original function implementation (we don't own the code) or it is more convenient to do so. It is a core technique used in functional programming and is facilitated by most of the functions in this subsection.

To demonstrate the _.bind() functionality, we will define an accumulator object with two methods, add(value) and substract(value), that will be extracted and invoked independently:

```
var accumulator = {
  currentValue: 0,
  add: function(value) {
    this.currentValue += value;
  },
  substract: function(value) {
    this.currentValue -= value;
  }
};

accumulator.currentValue = 5;
accumulator.add(2);
accumulator.substract(3);
console.log("accumulator.currentValue = " +
accumulator.currentValue);

var pseudoAccumulator1 = {
  currentValue: 1
};
var pseudoAccumulator2 = {
  currentValue: 2
};

var addFunction = _.bind(accumulator.add, pseudoAccumulator1);
var substractFunction = _.bind(accumulator.substract,
pseudoAccumulator2);

addFunction(2);
substractFunction(3);
console.log("pseudoAccumulator1.currentValue = " + pseudoAccumulator1.
currentValue);
console.log("pseudoAccumulator2.currentValue = " + pseudoAccumulator2.
currentValue);
// -> accumulator.currentValue = 4
//    pseudoAccumulator1.currentValue = 3
//    pseudoAccumulator2.currentValue = -1
```

 The _.bind() function is defined in the ES5 standard and Underscore will default to the native function if available.

A function closely related to `_.bind()` is `_.bindAll(object, *methodNames)`, where `*methodNames` is a list of function name parameters that belong to the `object` parameter (they are method names for the `object` parameter). This function ensures that all methods specified through the `methodNames` parameter have the `this` value set to the `object` parameter. It is useful when used in the context of event handlers, and in the following example, we will reuse the accumulator object and define two new methods, `add1()` and `substract1()`, that are suitable to be used as event handlers. Here is the HTML snippet that defines the example buttons:

```html
<button id="testBindAll_add1">Test _.bindAll() add1</button>
<br />
<button id="testBindAll_substract1">Test _.bindAll()
substract1</button>
<br />
<button id="testBindAll_log">Log accumulator.currentValue</button>
```

And here is the code that manipulates them:

```javascript
var accumulator = {
  currentValue: 0,
  add: function(value) {
    this.currentValue += value;
  },
  substract: function(value) {
    this.currentValue -= value;
  },
  add1: function() {
    this.currentValue += 1;
  },
  substract1: function() {
    this.currentValue -= 1;
  }
};

accumulator.currentValue = 5;
accumulator.add(2);
accumulator.substract(3);
console.log("accumulator.currentValue = " + accumulator.currentValue);

_.bindAll(accumulator, 'add1', 'substract1');

testBindAll_add1.addEventListener('click', accumulator.add1);

_.bindAll(accumulator, 'add1', 'substract1');
```

```
testBindAll_substract1.addEventListener('click',
accumulator.substract1);


testBindAll_log.addEventListener('click', function() {
  console.log("accumulator.currentValue = " +
  accumulator.currentValue);
});
```

If we remove the highlighted `_.bindAll()` line, `accumulator.currentValue` remains unchanged, and you can test this change using the online example at `http://bit.ly/1NekLkz`. The example output is written in the browser console.

Another function closely related to `_.bind()` is `_.partial(function, *arguments)`, which accomplishes the same functionality as the former function apart from presetting the `this` value. In addition, if any of the `*arguments` parameters is specified as `_`, it will leave that argument unset so that it can be replaced with a value specified when the result function is invoked (we should not mistake this argument with the Underscore global object). The approach facilitated by `_.partial()` is called **partial function application** and it is another frequently used functional programming technique.

We will revisit the `propertyFormatter.js` file and implement a function that uses the existing `extractDataPropertiesForDisplayAsArray` function to provide the same functionality for any object regardless of whether they have an `id` property or not. The new function `extractDataPropertiesForDisplayForAnyObject` has a signature with only one parameter, as shown in the next example that is a shortened version of the full `propertyFormatter.js` file:

```
var propertyFormatter = (function() {
  "use strict";

  var extractDataPropertiesForDisplayAsArray = function(source,
  ignoreId) {
    var propertiesForDisplay = [];
    if (_.isNull(source) || _.isUndefined(source) ||
_.isEmpty(source) || (!ignoreId && !_.isNumber(source.id))) {
      return propertiesForDisplay;
    }
    _.each(_.pairs(source), function(keyValue) {
      var key = keyValue[0];
      var value = keyValue[1];
      if (_.isDate(value) || _.isBoolean(value) ||
_.isNumber(value) || _.isString(value)) {
        propertiesForDisplay.push("Property '" + key + "' of type:
" + typeof value + " has value: " + value);
```

```
      } else if (!_.isFunction(value)) {
        propertiesForDisplay.push("Property: " + keyValue[0] + "
        cannot be displayed.");
      }
    });
    return propertiesForDisplay;
  };


  var extractDataPropertiesForDisplayForAnyObject =
  _.partial(extractDataPropertiesForDisplayAsArray, _, true);
  return {
    ...
    extractDataPropertiesForDisplayAsArray:
    extractDataPropertiesForDisplayAsArray,
    extractDataPropertiesForDisplayForAnyObject:
    extractDataPropertiesForDisplayForAnyObject,
    ...
  };
}());
```

The highlighted code demonstrates the use of the _.partial() function using the _ parameter. This parameter allows for the source value to be supplied when extractDataPropertiesForDisplayForAnyObject is invoked providing a simpler and elegant alternative for extractDataPropertiesForDisplayAsArray.

You can find the examples from this section within the functions folder from the source code for this chapter.

Further functional composition with memoize, wrap, negate, and compose

Underscore provides a powerful performance optimization through the use of the function _.memoize(function, [hashFunction]). By using this function, we can memorize the results of function calls using a default key set to the first function parameter value. Using _.memoize() creates a function that returns a memorized result each time it is called again with the same value for its first argument. When the arguments list is more complex, you can use the optional hashFunction parameter, where you define the key that will be used to store the function result based on the current arguments list.

The _.wrap(function, wrapper) function creates a function that can execute code before and after the function parameter is invoked. It enhances the functionality provided by the function parameter with additional code and it is another useful tool for functional composition.

To illustrate the power of `_.wrap()`, we will adapt the code from `index.js` that displays the example output in the browser to use this function. We will create a modified version of `propertyFormatter.extractPropertiesForDisplayAsArray` that adds a string to the result with information on the number of processed properties:

```
$(document).ready(function() {
  ...
  var extractPropertiesForDisplayWithFinalPropertiesCount = _.wrap(
    propertyFormatter.extractPropertiesForDisplayAsArray,
    function(func) {
      return function() {
        var result = func.apply(this, arguments);
        result.push("Processed property count is " + result.length
        + ".");
        return result;
      };
    })();

  var propertiesForDisplay =
  extractPropertiesForDisplayWithFinalPropertiesCount(source);

  $("#output").html("<h2>Object properties using a _.wrap version
  of propertyFormatter.extractPropertiesForDisplayAsArray:</h2>");

  _.each(propertiesForDisplay, function(line) {
    var existingContent = $("#output").html();
    $("#output").html(existingContent + "<br />" + line);
  });
  ...
});
```

The highlighted code creates a function that has a similar signature to `propertyFormatter.extractPropertiesForDisplayAsArray` with a slightly different result. You can use the example to experiment with versions that log how fast the original function took to execute or how many times it was called.

The `_.negate(predicate)` function returns the logical complement (negation) of the `predicate` function parameter and provides an elegant way to reuse an existing function that returns a Boolean result.

The `_.compose(*functions)` function takes one or more function parameters that will be evaluated from the last one to the first one with each function parameter receiving the result of the following function.

Controlling when and how often functions are called

Underscore provides a series of functions that manipulate the built-in JavaScript `setTimeout()` function to control when a function is called using a declarative approach.

The first function is `_.delay(function, wait, *arguments)` and it will invoke the `function` parameter after `wait` milliseconds using the parameters provided in the `*arguments` values. The second function, `_.defer(function, *arguments)`, is closely related, and it is useful when using Underscore in a complex computational context. The `function` parameter will be invoked only when the current call stack is clear, and thus, it will not be affected even if the actual `function` call is a computational heavy operation.

The next function, `_.throttle(function, wait, [options])`, returns a function that will invoke the `function` parameter at most once every `wait` milliseconds. This is useful when the result function will be called many times during `wait` milliseconds, and we need to limit the actual execution to one call for that duration. The initial function invocation is immediate, but if you pass `{leading: false}` as the optional `options` parameter the initial invocation will be done after the `wait` duration. Similarly, if `{trailing: false}` is passed, the `function` parameter will be invoked at the beginning of the `wait` duration rather than at the end as default. To demonstrate the functionality of `_.throttle()`, we have an example where we create a throttled function that, although called millions of times in the space of 6 seconds, it is actually only executed 3 times:

```
var throttledFunctionCallLimit = 3;
var throttledFunction = _.throttle(function() {
  console.log("Throttled function executed at: " + new Date());
  throttledFunctionCallLimit -= 1;
}, 2000, {
  leading: false
});
var i = 0;
while (throttledFunctionCallLimit > 0) {
  throttledFunction();
  i += 1;
}
console.log("The throttled function was called " + i + " times.");
// -> Throttled function executed at: Sun Sep 06 2015 13:50:15
//    Throttled function executed at: Sun Sep 06 2015 13:50:17
//    Throttled function executed at: Sun Sep 06 2015 13:50:19
//    The throttled function was called 31192639 times.
```

The last function based on setTimeout() is _.debounce(function, wait, [immediate]) that creates a wrapper function for the function parameter that will execute it after a delay of wait milliseconds since the wrapper function was last called. We will illustrate this function using a slightly more advanced example than the one for the _.throttle() function. Rather than using a while loop, we will recursively call a function that uses _.delay() to ensure the function created using _.debounce() has executed:

```
var debouncedFunctionCallLimit = 3;
var debouncedFunction = _.debounce(function() {
  console.log("Debounced function executed at: " + new Date());
  debouncedFunctionCallLimit -= 1;
}, 1000);
var i = 0;
var callDebouncedFunction = function() {
  if (debouncedFunctionCallLimit === 0) {
    console.log("The debounced function was called " + i + " times
    in total.");
    return;
  }
  debouncedFunction();
  debouncedFunction();
  debouncedFunction();
  debouncedFunction();
  debouncedFunction();
  i += 5;
  console.log("Called the debounced function 5 times in the
  current iteration.");
  _.delay(function() {
    callDebouncedFunction();
  }, 1500);
};
callDebouncedFunction();
// -> Called the debounced function 5 times in the current
//    iteration.
//    Debounced function executed at: Sun Sep 06 2015 16:43:32
//    Called the debounced function 5 times in the current
//    iteration.
//    Debounced function executed at: Sun Sep 06 2015 16:43:34
//    Called the debounced function 5 times in the current
//    iteration.
//    Debounced function executed at: Sun Sep 06 2015 16:43:35
//    The debounced function was called 15 times in total.
```

We try to call the function returned by `_.debounce()` 5 times, and then we wait 1.5 seconds before trying it to call it again, giving it the required one-second wait that it needs before it is executed.

The next set of functions control how many times a given function can be executed. The first function is `_.once(function)`, which creates a new function that ensures `function` is invoked once and only once. Each time the returned function is called, it will return the result of this first `function` invocation.

The next function is `_.after(count, function)`, which returns a function that when called repeatedly will only invoke the `function` parameter after it is called at least `count` times.

The last function of this subsection is `_.before(count, function)`, which returns a function that ensures that the `function` parameter will be invoked at most `count` times (it behaves like `_.once()` if `count` is 1). After the maximum number of calls is reached, each subsequent call will return the result of the last actual `function` invocation.

Utility functions

Underscore has a set of miscellaneous functions that we will enumerate briefly in this section. Some of these functions will be explored in other chapters, and they will have a summary description followed by the chapter reference:

- `_.noConflict()`: This returns the Underscore object when the `_` global variable is already in use
- `_.identity(value)`: This is mainly used by Underscore internally to return the `value` parameter as a result
- `_.constant(value)`: This is closely related to `_.identity()` and creates a function that returns the `value` parameter when invoked
- `_.noop()`: This creates a function that will always return `undefined` regardless of its invocation parameters
- `_.times(n, iteratee, [context])`: This invokes the `iteratee` function n times and each time it is passing the current invocation index as parameter; the result is an array with all the `iteratee` invocation return values
- `_.random(min, max)`: This returns a random integer between `min` and `max`
- `_.mixin(object)`: This provides a convenient way to add functionality to the Underscore object, and we will explore it further in *Chapter 6, Related Underscore.js Libraries and ECMAScript Standards*

- `_.iteratee(value, [context], [argCount])`: This is another Underscore internal function used to create functions that can be invoked against collection elements

- `_.uniqueId([prefix])`: This generates unique values using an Underscore internal counter and the optional `prefix` string parameter

- `_.escape(string)`, `_.unescape(string)`: The first function converts the characters &, <, >, ", ', and ` into their HTML escaped versions: &, <, >, ", ', and ` the second function performs the reverse operation

- `_.result(object, property)`: If `property` is a function property of `object`, it will be invoked and the result will be returned. If `property` is a value property of `object`, then the property value will be returned

- `_.now()`: This defaults to the native JavaScript `Date.now()` in an ES5 runtime; otherwise, it provides a faster replacement for older JavaScript runtimes

- `_.template(templateString, [settings])`: This provides HTML templating functionality; we will explore this function in *Chapter 5, Using Underscore.js in the Browser, on the Server, and with the Database.*

Summary

This chapter explored the specialized Underscore functions that target arrays, objects and functions. It also included a section on miscellaneous Underscore functions that will be referenced in other chapters.

The sections on objects and functions are a prerequisite for the next chapter that will discuss more about using programming paradigms with Underscore.

4

Programming Paradigms with Underscore.js

The previous chapter concluded the overview of most of the Underscore features. This chapter will explore how Underscore can be used in the context of different programming paradigms and has the following sections:

- An overview of the **object-oriented programming** (OOP) paradigm
- Examples of how you can use Underscore in an OOP context
- A description of the **functional programming** (FP) paradigm
- Examples of how you can use Underscore in a FP context

The chapter assumes that you are familiar with OOP concepts in general. In this chapter, we will use the programming paradigm interchangeable with the programming style.

The source code for the examples from this chapter is hosted online at `https://github.com/popalexandruvasile/underscorejs-examples/tree/master/programming-paradigms`, and you can execute the examples using the Cloud9 IDE at the address `https://ide.c9.io/alexpop/underscorejs-examples` from the `programming-paradigms` folder.

The object-oriented programming paradigm

JavaScript is a dynamic multi-paradigm programming language that can be used with an imperative, object-oriented, or functional programming style. Imperative programming is a programming style found in languages that can be used for scripting, and we will explore this style in *Chapter 5, Using Underscore.js in the Browser, on the Server, and with the Database.*

Object-oriented programming is mainly characterized by the use of objects created using classes in class-based languages or cloned from other objects in prototype-based languages. Some of the object-oriented features are abstraction, inheritance, polymorphism, encapsulation, and information hiding, and these features favor a programming style where objects contain both data and behavior represented by methods.

 You can find more OOP principles and patterns described in the "Gang of four" design patterns at https://en.wikipedia.org/wiki/ Software_design_pattern and the S.O.L.I.D. principles at http:// www.butunclebob.com/ArticleS.UncleBob.PrinciplesOfOod.

The JavaScript language facilitates object-oriented features through its built in prototypal inheritance. Each object is either of the built-in type `Object` or inherits from it directly or indirectly through **prototypal inheritance**. Although this concept might be a bit more advanced for some developers, I think it is essential to explore it at the beginning of this section because:

- Prototypal inheritance is a key mechanism to share data and behavior between JavaScript objects
- Underscore provides a couple of functions that facilitate and simplify prototypal inheritance
- ES6 introduces classes with a syntax that is similar with class-based languages, but prototypal inheritance is still being used under-the-covers

In the ECMAScript specification, each object has an internal built-in property defined as `[[Prototype]]` and implemented initially by browser vendors as a nonstandard property called `__proto__`. ES5 defined a standard function called `Object.getPrototypeOf(obj)` that returns the `[[Prototype]]` value for an object and ES6 went further and standardized the `__proto__` property. Using either of the two approaches will return the same `[[Prototype]]` value, and we will refer to it as the **object prototype** from now on.

Understanding prototypal inheritance can prove difficult for programmers coming from OOP languages with class-based inheritance. In JavaScript, objects inherit from instances of other objects and share properties via the object prototype. In this section, we will use a series of examples that explore these concepts via a bare-bones project structure for a better focus.

Inheritance with object literals

The first example demonstrates that all object literals are bound to the same prototype that is the built-in default JavaScript `Object` prototype. We will take a simplified version of the client object from our bicycles-related samples, and we will make two objects out of it (one inheriting from the other). The initial object is similar to the contact object we used in previous examples:

```
var originalClient = {
  "id": 1,
  "name": "Baxter Brooks",
  "gender": "male",
  "type": "client",
  "email": "baxterbrooks@dymi.com",
  "registered": "2014-03-15T10:52:05 -00:00",
  "isActive": false,
};
var contact = {
  "id": 1,
  "name": "Baxter Brooks",
  "gender": "male",
  "type": "contact",
  "email": "baxterbrooks@dymi.com",
};
var assertObjectLiteralPrototype = originalClient.__proto__ ===
contact.__proto__ && contact.__proto__ === {}.__proto__;
console.log(exampleTitle + "Assert that the default [[Prototype]]
property of any object literal is the same object instance: " +
assertObjectLiteralPrototype);
```

The highlighted code snippet is accessing the `[[Protoype]]` property defined in the ECMAScript specification using the `contact.__proto__` property (available in any modern browser). The same expression can be rewritten so it is strictly ES5 compliant:

```
Object.getPrototypeOf(originalClient) ===
Object.getPrototypeOf(contact) && Object.getPrototypeOf(contact)
=== Object.getPrototypeOf({})
```

I prefer the `__proto__` notation as it is more expressive and succinct and it is now part of the ES6 standard. It proves useful when invoked in the browser JavaScript console although it should not be used in the production code.

You can execute the examples from this section at `http://bit.ly/1KfBLSb` or from the folder `oop-inheritance` from the source code for this chapter. The first series of examples can be found in the `inheritanceUsingObjectLiterals.js` file.

We will now create a new `client1` object that is set to inherit from the `contact` object by setting the `[[Protoype]]` property of the former to the instance of the latter:

```
var client1 = {
  __proto__: contact,
  "type": "client",
  "registered": "2014-03-15T10:52:05 -00:00",
  "isActive": false,
};
var assertClient1Prototype = client1.__proto__ ===
Object.getPrototypeOf(client1) && client1.__proto__ === contact;
console.log(exampleTitle + "Assert that [[Prototype]] for object
'client1' is 'contact': " + assertClient1Prototype);
```

If you inspect the `client1` object when you execute the example, you will notice that it has all the property values of `contact`, for example, `client1.id`, with the exception of the `type` property that was overwritten. This example represents the simplest case of a prototypal inheritance chain — when we access a property on an object that is not defined on the same object, the JavaScript runtime will inspect the object prototype and look for the property there. This is a recursive process that will stop after the default object literal prototype is reached, as its own prototype is `null` (this can be expressed in the code as `{}.__proto__.__proto__ === null`).

The previous example can be also written as ES5-compliant code using the built-in `Object.create()` function and `_.extend()`:

```
var client2 = Object.create(contact);
_.extend(client2, {
  "type": "client",
  "registered": "2014-03-15T10:52:05 -00:00",
  "preferredBike": "A clown bike",
  "isActive": false,
});
var assertClient2Prototype = client2.__proto__ ===
Object.getPrototypeOf(client2) && client2.__proto__ === contact;
```

```
console.log(exampleTitle + "Assert that [[Prototype]] for object
'client2' is 'contact': " + assertClient2Prototype);
```

The function `Object.create(proto[, propertiesObject])` will create a new object instance with its `[[Prototype]]` property set to `proto` and additional properties defined through the optional `propertiesObject` object.

Underscore provides a simpler alternative to the `Object.create()` function and this is `_.create(prototype, props)`. The previous code snippet can use the `_.create()` function instead of both `Object.create()` and `_.extend()`:

```
var client2 = _.create(contact, {
  "type": "client",
  "registered": "2014-03-15T10:52:05 -00:00",
  "preferredBike": "A clown bike",
  "isActive": false,
});
```

As `client1` and `client2` objects share the same `contact` prototype, we can add new properties for all these objects when we set them as `contact.__proto__` properties:

```
client1.__proto__.emailSubscriber = true;
console.log(exampleTitle + "Assert that all objects inheriting
from 'contact' and 'contact' itself have emailSubscriber set to
true: " + (contact.emailSubscriber && client1.emailSubscriber &&
client2.emailSubscriber));

client1.__proto__.getContactIdAndName = function() {
  return this.name + " (" + this.id + ")";
};
console.log(exampleTitle + "Assert that all objects inheriting
from 'contact' and 'contact' itself have the same value for
getContactIdAndName(): " + (contact.getContactIdAndName() ===
client1.getContactIdAndName() && contact.getContactIdAndName() ===
client2.getContactIdAndName()));
```

The example represents the simplest form of extending objects with new functionality. In theory, we can use the `contact` prototype to add new properties. Because the `contact` prototype is the built-in default JavaScript `Object` prototype, we will also extend all JavaScript objects, which can potentially break any code relying on these objects behaving as per the ECMAScript standard. Extending built-in JavaScript prototypes is considered a bad practice unless used in libraries that implement unsupported JavaScript features for older browsers (these libraries are also known as **polyfills**).

Inheritance with object constructors

The second series of examples explores a different way to create objects that allows for more control and flexibility compared to using object literals.

In JavaScript, a function becomes an **object constructor** function when used with the new operator. Calling a function with the new operator will create a new object instance, and you can reference the new instance in the constructor function body via the built-in this variable.

The object literal-based example is adapted to use an object constructor and calling the object constructor creates the contact instance:

```
function Contact(id, name, gender, email) {
  this.id = id;
  this.name = name;
  this.gender = gender;
  this.type = "contact";
  this.email = email;
}
var contact = new Contact(
  1,
  "Baxter Brooks",
  "male",
  "baxterbrooks@dymi.com"
);
```

The convention for the object constructor is to use Pascal cased names as Contact to keep the syntax close to similar syntax in OOP languages with class-based inheritance.

The last line of the code snippet is identical with calling a class constructor in an OOP language such as C#; the example demonstrates how a class definition and instantiation looks like in JavaScript.

The contact object has a property called constructor, which points to the Contact function. To check whether an object is a specific "class" in OOP terminology, we can check its constructor properties like in the expression: contact.constructor. name === "Contact". I should note that this check is simplistic and it does not cover cases such as the Array type that has a different kind of constructor. A better way to check that an object is of a specific type is to use the JavaScript operator instanceof, which can be used in an expression such as: contact instanceof Contact === true. The operator checks whether an object inherits directly or indirectly from a constructor function prototype.

Other important advantages to using an object constructor function are as follows:

- A constructor function has a built-in property called `prototype` that holds the `[[Prototype]]` property of all the object instances created with it

- A constructor function `prototype` property is unique and different from the built-in default JavaScript `Object` prototype

The next example contains an expression that verifies the `contact` object prototype assumptions using the __proto__ property first and the `instanceof` operator second:

```
console.log(exampleTitle + "Assert that [[Prototype]] for
'contact' instance is the object constructor prototype: " +
(contact.__proto__ === Contact.prototype));
var assertContactIsInstanceOfContact = contact instanceof Contact;
console.log(exampleTitle + "Assert that 'contact' is an instance
of Contact: " + assertContactIsInstanceOfContact);
```

Using object constructors, we can validate object properties before an instance is created, and we have a unique object prototype that can be used to extend behavior in a safe way.

We will now revisit the object literal representing a client and change it to use inheritance based on object constructors. First, we will define a `Client` object constructor that creates objects with a prototype that inherits from `Contact.prototype`:

```
function Client(id, name, gender, email, registered, isActive) {
  Contact.call(this, id, name, gender, email);
  this.type = 'client';
  this.registered = registered;
  this.isActive = isActive;
}
Client.prototype = Object.create(Contact.prototype);
Client.prototype.constructor = Client;

var client = new Client(
  1,
  "Baxter Brooks",
  "male",
  "baxterbrooks@dymi.com",
  "2014-03-15T10:52:05 -00:00",
  false
);
```

Within the `Client` constructor function, we are calling the `Contact` constructor to initialize all inherited properties with the exception of the `type` property and set the `Client` specific properties after that.

The first line of the highlighted code should be familiar as it is similar to the `Object.create()` invocation from the inheritance with object literals example. This time around we use it to ensure the `Client` prototype inherits from the `Contact` prototype. The effect of using this line is the same as before with the distinction that now the two prototypes are unique and distinct and can be accessed using simpler code. Having a common and easy to access prototype allows us to extend the functionality of all `Contact` and `Client` instances in a controlled, flexible, and elegant manner. The last highlighted line links the `Client` prototype constructor (which holds the `Contact` constructor function at this point) with the `Client` constructor function, completing the last piece of infrastructure for implementing prototypal inheritance with object constructors.

We can verify the relationship between object prototypes with this expression:

```
console.log(exampleTitle + "Assert that [[Prototype]] for 'client'
inherits from the [[Prototype]] for 'contact': " +
(client.__proto__.__proto__ === contact.__proto__));
```

Another way to verify this relationship is to use the `instanceof` operator:

```
var assertClientIsInstanceOfContact = client instanceof Contact;
console.log(exampleTitle + "Assert that 'client' is an instance
of Contact: " + assertClientIsInstanceOfContact);
```

The next step is to extend both `Contact` and `Client` object functionality through `Contact.prototype`:

```
Contact.prototype.getContactIdAndName = function() {
  return this.name + " (" + this.id + ")";
};
console.log(exampleTitle + "Assert that all objects inheriting
from 'Contact' or that are 'Contact' have the same value for
getContactIdAndName(): " + (contact.getContactIdAndName() ===
client.getContactIdAndName()));
```

We will start referring to object constructors as classes from now to make their intent more explicit for readers with an OOP background and we will expand this subject when we discuss ES6 classes.

In this subsection, we explored OOP features based on ES5 and we will discuss more about OOP improvements in ES6 in *Chapter 6, Related Underscore.js Libraries and ECMAScript Standards*.

JavaScript support for OOP is more extensive than was explored in this section. You can find more information about OOP and JavaScript on the Mozilla Developer Network website at `https://developer.mozilla.org/en-US/docs/Web/JavaScript/Introduction_to_Object-Oriented_JavaScript` and `https://developer.mozilla.org/en-US/docs/Web/JavaScript/Inheritance_and_the_prototype_chain`. I also recommend a book that I found especially useful and it is available to read online at `http://eloquentjavascript.net/` — see *Chapter 6, The Secret Life Of Objects*.

Using Underscore with the object-oriented programming paradigm

In this chapter, we used functions such as `_.extend()` and `_.create()` that helped us leverage prototypal inheritance. We will now walkthrough some code examples that showcase various Underscore functions that facilitate the OOP paradigm.

Using classes with original client data

We will start a series of examples that build upon the prototypal inheritance and are based on the previous chapter's sample data. The leading requirement that we need to implement is to differentiate between active clients (referred to as clients) and inactive ones (referred to as contacts). To make this distinction, we will use the property isActive of the original client object, and we will retrieve just contact-related properties for the inactive clients.

First, we will extend the object constructors introduced in this chapter for the Contact and Client objects to include all the properties that were removed for brevity. You can find the two constructor functions in the classes.js file in the oop-underscore folder from the source code for this chapter.

Next, we will change the clientRetriever.js file so that it loads the original client objects returned by dataRetriever.getClients() into an array of Contact and Client instances:

```
var clientRetriever = (function() {
  "use strict";
  var getContacts = function() {
    var clientObjects = dataProvider.getClients();
    return _.map(clientObjects, function(clientObject) {
```

```
        if (!clientObject.isActive) {
          return new Contact(
            clientObject.id,
            clientObject.name,
            clientObject.gender,
            clientObject.company,
            clientObject.email,
            clientObject.phone,
            clientObject.address);
        }
        return new Client(
          clientObject.id,
          clientObject.name,
          clientObject.gender,
          clientObject.company,
          clientObject.email,
          clientObject.phone,
          clientObject.address,
          new Date(clientObject.registered),
          clientObject.preferredBike,
          clientObject.bikePoints,
          clientObject.notes
        );
      });
    };
    return {
      getContacts: getContacts
    };
  }());
```

If an original client object has the isActive property set to true, we create a
Client object; if not, we create a Contact object. Because Client inherits
from Contact, any Client object is also a Contact object, so the main function
is called getContacts() to reflect the common denominator.

 It is worth mentioning that the constructor functions Contact()
and Client() from the classes.js file could be refactored to
accept an object argument that has all the required properties for
the constructed object.

Based upon these changes we can now create a function to retrieve the active clients
represented by the Client type. We have multiple ways to accomplish this: by
comparing the type property, by comparing the object constructor type, and by
using the instanceof operator.

We will implement all three functions in the `clientRetriever.js` file:

```
getClientsUsingTypeProperty: function() {
  var contacts = getContacts();
  return _.filter(contacts, function(contact) {
    return contact.type === "client";
  });
},
getClientsUsingConstructorType: function() {
  var contacts = getContacts();
  return _.filter(contacts, function(contact) {
    return contact.constructor === Client;
  });
},
getClientsUsingInstanceof: function() {
  var contacts = getContacts();
  return _.filter(contacts, function(contact) {
    return contact instanceof Client;
  });
}
```

The last function gives us an elegant and expressive way to ensure an object is of a specific type and we verify that all functions return the same results in the associated test specifications from the `spec/clientRetrieverSpec.js` file.

Constructor validation with Underscore

One of the advantages of using object constructors is that we can control the creation of objects via validation. In *Chapter 3, Using Underscore.js with Arrays, Objects, and Functions,* we explored a series of functions such as `_.isNumber()` and `_.isString()` that can be used to make type assertions against an object. We also discussed the function `_.toArray()` that transforms the `arguments` variable available in any JavaScript function into an array for convenient manipulation. We will use the latter function first to validate that the object constructor has the correct number of arguments and the former ones to validate that the arguments are of the correct type. This is the changed implementation for the `Contact` class in `classes.js`:

```
var Contact = (function() {
  "use strict";
  function Contact(id, name, gender, company, email, phone,
  address) {
    var argsArray = _.toArray(arguments);
    if (argsArray.length != 7) {
      throw {
        name: "ArgumentsException",
```

```
          message: "The arguments length is incorrect."
        };
      }
      if (!_.isNumber(id) || !_.isString(name) ||
      !_.isString(gender) || !_.isString(company) ||
      !_.isString(email) || !_.isString(phone) ||
      !_.isString(address)) {
        throw {
          name: "ArgumentsException",
          message: "One of the arguments does not have the expected
          type."
        };
      }
      this.id = id;
      this.name = name;
      this.gender = gender;
      this.company = company;
      this.email = email;
      this.phone = phone;
      this.address = address;
      this.type = "contact";
    }
    Contact.prototype.getContactNameIdAndType = function() {
      return this.name + " (" + this.id + " - " + this.type + ")";
    };
    return Contact;
}());
```

Any validation error will be thrown as an exception so, when we write the test specifications for our class in the `spec/contactSpec.js` file, we need to use a slightly different syntax. We define a function variable that creates an invalid `Contact`
object, and then we check that the exact exception name and message were thrown:

```
describe("Given Client class", function() {
  describe("when calling new Client() with too few arguments",
  function() {
    var createClient = function() {
      new Client(1, " A contact name");
    };
    it("then throws the correct exception", function() {
      expect(createClient).toThrow({
        name: 'ArgumentsException',
        message: 'The arguments length is incorrect.'
      });
```

```
    });
  });
  describe("when calling new Client() with an argument of the
  wrong type", function() {
    var createClient = function() {
      new Client(1, " A contact name", "Female", "Company2", "An
      email", "Phone1", "An address",
        "Date2014", "A bike", 200, "Some notes ");
    };
    it("then throws the correct exception", function() {
      expect(createClient).toThrow({
        name: "ArgumentsException",
        message: "One of the arguments does not have the expected
        type."
      });
    });
  });
});
```

You can find the validation changes for the Client class in the classes.js file and the tests specs in the spec/clientSpec.js file.

The Underscore object-related functions helped us build a class implementation that should feel familiar to developers coming from a class-based OOP language. The example also demonstrates that, even if Underscore is implemented in a functional programming style, this does not mean it can't be used in an OOP context. You can use it as a general-purpose utility library rather than as a functional library although it will prove to be a solid base to build your own functional code, as discussed in the rest of the chapter.

The functional programming paradigm

In the first chapter, we described a couple of the principles behind the functional programming paradigm. Underscore in itself is a great example of applying functional programming in JavaScript while the jQuery library also observes functional programming principles.

Up until the current chapter, all the examples tried to remain close to functional programming principles and you already saw some of these principles in action:

- Using functions as first-class citizens in most of the examples
- Using objects as data structures while relying on standalone functions (as opposed to object methods) for implementing functionality in most of the examples

- Using higher-order functions and immutability in the collections and arrays examples
- Functional composition in the functions examples

Alongside immutability an important concept in functional programming is using functions that don't have side effects. These are functions that do not modify the global state or outside state, do not modify their arguments and if called with the same arguments, they return the same results. You can find this concept applied in most of the examples discussed up until and including this chapter.

We will explore another concept that straddles the demarcation line between OOP and FP paradigms. The concept is known as **method chaining** and it is a programming technique where object method calls can be chained together if they return either the same instance of an object or the same type of object.

We will revisit the first example from the first chapter and use the built in `Array` methods `map`, `filter`, and `reduce` to calculate the bicycle count using method chaining:

```
var bicycles = [{
name: "A fast bike",
type: "Road Bike"
}, {
...
}, {
name: "A clown bike",
type: "Children Bike"
}];
var bicycleTypeCountData = bicycles
.map(function(bicycle) {
  return bicycle.type;
})
.filter(function(bicycleType) {
  return bicycleType !== 'Children Bike';
})
.reduce(function(bicycleTypeCount, bicycleType) {
  bicycleTypeCount[bicycleType] += 1;
  return bicycleTypeCount;
}, {
  "Road Bike": 0,
  "Mountain Bike": 0,
  "Urban Bike": 0
});
//=> Chaining using arrays : {"Road Bike":2,"Mountain
Bike":3,"Urban Bike":2}
```

We started by calling the first method on an `Array` instance and stopped with the final call that returned an `Object` instance, breaking the method chain. Underscore also has built in support for method chaining and we will explore it in the final section of this chapter.

You can find the example in the `chaining.js` file under the `fp` folder from the source code for this chapter.

Adopting a functional programming style does not mean you necessarily have to forego classes. As long as the classes are describing a data structure rather than encapsulating behavior, they can be used with a functional programming style as demonstrated in the next section. We will explore more functional programming features in *Chapter 6, Related Underscore.js Libraries and ECMAScript Standards*, when we discuss the library `underscore-contrib`.

 The topic of functional programming in JavaScript is extensive and you can find more information in *Functional JavaScript, Michael Fogus, O'Reilly Media*, 2013 and in *JavaScript Allongé* by Reginald Braithwaite available to read online at `https://leanpub.com/javascript-allonge/read`—to name just a few of the resources available on this topic.

Migrating to a functional programming style

We will revisit the examples in the folder `oop-underscore` from the source code for this chapter and adapt them to use standalone functions instead of object methods:

- We will keep the classes as simple data structures and we will even preserve the inheritance
- We will move all the functionality around validation and any object methods outside the original classes

Because we want to preserve the existing functionality, we will leave the test specifications unchanged together with the code that displays the example output. First of all, we will move the validation logic into a separate `validations.js` file. The object constructor functions for `Contact` and `Client` are validating the argument's length and we will move this functionality into a new function:

```
validateArgsLength: function(argsLength, argsArray) {
  if (argsArray.length != argsLength) {
    throw {
```

```
        name: "ArgumentsException",
        message: "The arguments length is incorrect."
      };
    }
  }
```

The second validation done in both object constructors was for the argument types. We will replace this validation with a set of new functions, as shown in the next code snippet:

```
validateArgsTypes: function(argsArray, argumentValidatorArray) {
  _.each(argsArray, function(argument, index) {
    if (!argumentValidatorArray[index](argument)) {
      throw {
        name: "ArgumentsException",
        message: "One of the arguments does not have the expected
        type."
      };
    }
  });
},
validateContactArgs: function(argsArray) {
  this.validateArgsTypes(
    argsArray, [_.isNumber, _.isString, _.isString, _.isString,
    _.isString, _.isString, _.isString]);
},
validateClientArgs: function(argsArray) {
  this.validateContactArgs(_.first(argsArray, 7));
  this.validateArgsTypes(
    _.rest(argsArray, 7), [_.isDate, _.isString, _.isNumber,
    _.isString]);
}
```

The first new function `validateArgsTypes()` is used by the object-specific validators `validateContactArgs()` and `validateClientArgs()`, and we have used Underscore functions to split the arguments array. We can also highlight the usefulness of manipulating function arguments through the array created by the `_.toArray()` function. We can use the arguments with the Underscore array functions `_.first()` and `_.rest()`, which would not be possible if we left them unchanged.

The `Contact` class definition is a lot simpler now:

```
var Contact = (function() {
  "use strict";
  function Contact(id, name, gender, company, email, phone,
  address) {
```

```
      var argsArray = _.toArray(arguments);
      validations.validateArgsLength(7, argsArray);
      validations.validateContactArgs(argsArray);
      this.id = id;
      this.name = name;
      this.gender = gender;
      this.company = company;
      this.email = email;
      this.phone = phone;
      this.address = address;
      this.type = "contact";
    }
    return Contact;
}());
```

The highlighted code shows the new validation function calls. The validations object is similar to other objects encapsulating functionality that we used in other examples such as clientRetriever and dataProvider. This object represents a unit of closely related functionality and represents a module. The concept of a JavaScript module will be explored in *Chapter 5, Using Underscore.js in the Browser, on the Server, and with the Database* and *Chapter 6, Related Underscore.js Libraries and ECMAScript Standards*.

We have similar replacement code for the validation logic in the Client class:

```
var Client = (function() {
  "use strict";
  function Client(id, name, gender, company, email, phone,
  address, registered, preferredBike, bikePoints, notes) {
    var argsArray = _.toArray(arguments);
    validations.validateArgsLength(11, argsArray);
    validations.validateClientArgs(argsArray);
    Contact.call(this, id, name, gender, company, email, phone,
    address);
    this.type = 'client';
    this.registered = registered;
    this.preferredBike = preferredBike;
    this.bikePoints = bikePoints;
    this.notes = notes;
  }
  Client.prototype = Object.create(Contact.prototype);
  Client.prototype.constructor = Client;
  return Client;
}());
```

We kept the code that implements the inheritance between the two classes unchanged but, if it is removed, it does not have any impact on our example. The two classes are still linked together and we moved the validation logic into a separate module. We can now reuse the validation logic in different contexts.

This refactoring is extended to the getNameIdAndType() function that was implemented in the Contact class and inherited by the Client class. We moved it into a separate module in the transformations.js file:

```
var transformations = (function() {
  "use strict";
  return {
    getContactNameIdAndType: function(contact) {
      return contact.name + " (" + contact.id + " - " +
      contact.type + ")";
    }
  };
}());
```

Similar to the validations objects, we now have access to the new function getContactNameIdAndType() in other contexts without having to create a Contact or Client instance first. This gives us greater flexibility and the ability to compose and expand existing functions outside the original classes' context.

You can even restore the Contact.getNameIdAndType() method by calling transformations.getContactNameIdAndType() in its implementation. This is where following strict FP principles and OOP principles can drive a class definition in different directions. I personally prefer to keep the programming style consistent and avoid mixing and matching different principles in the same module or class. As mentioned in the OOP section, you can use a functional library such as Underscore in an OOP context; however, the opposite might prove a bit of a stretch.

JavaScript is not a fully-fledged functional programming language and, while it has functional programming elements, it also has object-oriented constructs. You could easily create a codebase that supports both programming styles: FP for algorithms and data transformations and OOP for data persistence or rich user interface-related objects. This does not mean that you could not use FP for the entire codebase or that FP is more limited than OOP—many modern programming languages such as JavaScript are multi-paradigm languages, and it is up to the developer to choose the most appropriate style.

Functional programming with Underscore.js

In the previous chapter, we excluded some important functions that are essential in implementing the method-chaining concept. Underscore has built-in support for this concept through the _.chain(obj) function, which returns a new instance of the _ object with the obj parameter stored as a property of the returned object; this property is called _wrapped. The new _ instance is different from the global _ object exclusively used up until now in all our examples. The new _ instance becomes the vehicle of the method chain started with _.chain(obj) and we can use it to call any Underscore function without specifying the first argument. The first argument is always implied to be the _wrapped instance, so we can write code like this:

```
var people = [{
  name: "Herta Muller",
  birthYear: 1953,
  awardYear: 2009
}, {
  name: "Mario Vargas Llosa",
  birthYear: 1936,
  awardYear: 2010
}, {
  name: "Tomas Transtromer",
  birthYear: 1931,
  awardYear: 2011
}, {
  name: "Mo Yan",
  birthYear: 1955,
  awardYear: 2012
}, {
  name: "Alice Munro",
  birthYear: 1931,
  awardYear: 2013
}, {
  name: "Patrick Modiano",
  birthYear: 1945,
  awardYear: 2014
}];

var averagePersonAge = _.chain(people)
```

```
    .map(function(person) {
      return {
        name: person.name,
        awardAge: person.awardYear - person.birthYear
      };
    })
    .reduce(function(memo, person, index) {
      memo += person.awardAge;
      if (index === people.length - 1) {
        return Math.floor(memo / people.length);
      }
      return memo;
    }, 0)
    .value();
  //=> 69
```

We took the example from the `underscore.map.reduce` folder from the source code for the first chapter and we applied the method chaining concept using `_.chain()`. The last method call `value()` ends the method chain, returning the final `_wrapped` value shown in the last line of the code snippet representing the example output.

The third Underscore function used in method chaining is `_.tap(object, interceptor)`, which will invoke the `interceptor` function parameter with the `object` parameter passed as an argument. The function is useful when we need to access the intermediary result for a method chain. If we introduce the next code snippet between subsequent method chain calls, we will see the `_wrapped` value in the browser JavaScript console:

```
    .tap(function(result) {
      console.log(result);
    })
```

We can also call some of the built-in JavaScript `Array.prototype` functions as part of a method chain initiated with `_.chain()`: pop, push, reverse, shift, sort, splice, unshift, concat, join, and slice. This feature makes Underscore a great choice for manipulating arrays in general. Through the use of `_.chain()`, we effectively create a **fluent interface** for transforming data in a concise and expressive manner.

Another interesting feature of functional programming languages is **lazy evaluation**, where the value of an expression is calculated only when actually needed. JavaScript does not support lazy evaluation out of the box, but if it did we could visualize the `_.chain()` example, invoking all the methods only when the final method `value()` is called.

The practical value of a lazy evaluation language is the ability to further compose method chains and some multi-paradigm languages such as C# have support for this feature.

The extensive support for FP provided by Underscore can be used as a solid base on which to build a library in a functional style. There are other libraries built on Underscore, and we will explore them further in *Chapter 6, Related Underscore.js Libraries and ECMAScript Standards*.

Summary

In this chapter, we explored different programming paradigms that can be used with Underscore. Both the OOP and FP paradigms were discussed using code examples that highlighted the built-in JavaScript support first followed by expanded examples using Underscore.

The next chapter will present Underscore usage scenarios within specific environments: browser, server, and database.

5

Using Underscore.js in the Browser, on the Server, and with the Database

In the previous chapter, we discussed how to use Underscore in the context of two different programming paradigms and explored some of the programming principles behind OOP and FP using a series of code samples.

In this chapter, we will see Underscore in action, applied in separate contexts:

- In the browser with Underscore templates
- On the server with Node.js
- With the MongoDB and PostgreSQL databases

The chapter assumes that you know fundamental jQuery concepts and have some basic notions about web development and server-side and relational database programing in general.

The source code for the examples from this chapter is hosted online at `https://github.com/popalexandruvasile/underscorejs-examples/tree/master/browser-server-database`, and you can execute the examples using the Cloud9 IDE at the address `https://ide.c9.io/alexpop/underscorejs-examples` from the `browser-server-database` folder.

Using Underscore in the browser

In this section, we will explore Underscore browser-specific features. We will start by pulling most of the code developed for *Chapter 4, Programming Paradigms with Underscore.js*, from the `fp-underscore` folder and create an initial example with a focus on user interface changes. We will render the example output using a popular **frontend design framework** as a fast and efficient way to prototype web application.

Enhancing examples output with Bootstrap

In the last couple of years, the rise in JavaScript frameworks has been matched by a rise in frontend design frameworks such as Bootstrap and Foundation. These frameworks provide a consistent set of HTML markup and base CSS files that will render a user interface with a specific look and feel. You can customize this look and feel by providing your own version of the base CSS or use a prebuilt one. Frontend design frameworks have a central grid system that is used to layout and organize content. They also have support for implementing responsive web design with a lot of built-in functionality that will adapt the user interface for various screen sizes.

In this book, we will use the Bootstrap framework and, although an initial overview is provided, a good place to get more in-depth documentation is `http://getbootstrap.com`.

The Bootstrap grid system is based on a 12-column layout that is usually built with `div` tags and special CSS classes to differentiate between rows and columns. CSS classes are also used to set column widths, offsets, and spans. We will adapt the initial example found in the `browser-underscore` folder from the source code for this chapter and use Bootstrap to structure the rendered output. We need to add the Bower package that contains this framework by first running the following command in the example folder:

```
bower install bootstrap#3.3.4 --save
```

Next, we need to add a script reference to the base CSS file located at `bower_components/bootstrap/dist/css/bootstrap.css` from the Bootstrap Bower package.

If you browse the `index-original.html` file from the `browser-underscore` example folder, you will see that the example output is rendered using the Bootstrap framework:

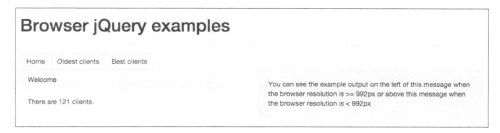

There is now an example output area on the left and an information message on the right. If the browser width drops below 992 px, the content gets aligned horizontally to fit devices with smaller screens and you will see the right message beneath the example output area. Here is the HTML markup with highlighted Bootstrap-specific elements:

```
<div class="container">
  <div class="row">
    <div class="col-md-12">
      <div class="page-header">
        <h1>Browser jQuery examples
        </h1>
      </div>
    </div>
  </div>
  <div class="row">
    <div class="col-md-12">
      <div class="btn-group">
        <button id="home-btn" type="button" class="btn btn-
        default">Home</button>
        <button id="oldest-clients-btn" type="button" class="btn
        btn-default">Oldest clients</button>
        <button id="best-clients-btn" type="button" class="btn
        btn-default">Best clients</button>
      </div>
    </div>
```

```
      </div>
      <div class="row">
        <div class="col-md-6">
          <div class="panel panel-default">
            <div class="panel-heading">Panel heading</div>
            <div class="panel-body">Panel body</div>
          </div>
        </div>
        <div class="col-md-6">
          <div class="well">
            You can see the example output on the left of this message
            when the browser resolution is &gt;= 992px or above this
            message when the browser resolution is &lt; 992px </div>
        </div>
      </div>
    </div>
```

The first highlighted attribute initializes the Bootstrap grid system with matching `class="row"` attributes and `class="col-md-12"` attributes that define the rows and cells of the grid. The first two rows have one cell each that spans the entire Bootstrap 12-column layout. The last row has two cells and each cell spans 6 grid columns as defined by the `class="col-md-6"` attribute. The `md` class name part instructs Bootstrap to collapse the two cells horizontally when the browser's horizontal resolution is less than 992 px. Because the first two rows contain only one cell, they will always show its content on a single line regardless of the browser resolution.

The first row defines a Bootstrap page header component through the `class="page-header"` attribute. The second row has a Bootstrap button group component defined by the `class="btn-group"` attribute. We use it as basic navigation for our example output and its buttons are used to trigger the display of different `clientRetriever` function call results, as shown in the `index-original.js` code:

```javascript
$(document).ready(function() {
  var oldestClients = clientRetriever.getOldestClients(5);
  var bestClients = clientRetriever.getBestClients(5);
  var clients = clientRetriever.getClients();
  var onSelectHome = function() {
    $(".panel-heading").html("Welcome");
    $(".panel-body").html("<p>There are " + clients.length + "
    clients.</p>");
  };
  $("#home-btn").click(onSelectHome);
  $("#oldest-clients-btn").click(function() {
```

```
$(".panel-heading").html("Top 5 oldest clients with name, id and
type");
var displayContent = "<ul><li>" +
  _.map(oldestClients, function(client) {
    return transformations.getContactNameIdAndType(client);
  }).join('</li><li>') +
  "</li></ul>";
$(".panel-body").html(displayContent);
});
$("#best-clients-btn").click(function() {
  $(".panel-heading").html("Top 5 best clients with name, id and
  type");
  var displayContent = "<ul><li>" +
    _.map(bestClients, function(client) {
      return transformations.getContactNameIdAndType(client);
    }).join('</li><li>') +
    "</li></ul>";
  $(".panel-body").html(displayContent);
});
onSelectHome();
});
```

On closer inspection, the code from the two highlighted `click` event handlers seems a bit repetitive, and we will use the templating support in Underscore to provide a better alternative.

Better HTML markup with Underscore templates

Underscore provides the `_.template(templateString, [settings])` function that takes an HTML string with special formatted snippets, which is provided in the `templateString` parameter, and returns a function. The function returned by `_.template()` should be invoked with an object that contains the properties referenced in the special formatted snippets as in the next examples.

The `templateString` parameter can contain the following:

- Expressions delimited by `<%= ... %>`, which are interpolated:
  ```
  var template = _.template("<h1><%= client.name %></h1>");
  template({ client: { name: "Evelyn Obrien" } });
  //=> "<h1>Evelyn Obrien</h1>"
  ```

- Expressions delimited `<% ... %>` that are evaluated as verbatim JavaScript code:

```
var template = _.template("<h1><% if(client.name) { %> <%=
client.name %> <% } else { %> N/A <% } %></h1>");
template({ client: {} });
//=> "<h1> N/A </h1>"
template({ client: { name: "Giles Sykes" } });
//=> "<h1>Giles Syke</h1>"
```

- Expressions delimited by `<%- ... %>`, which are interpolated and HTML-escaped:

```
var template = _.template("<h1><%- client.name %></h1>");
template({ client: { name: "A. & R. Thompson" } });
//=> "<h1>A. &amp; R. Thompson</h1>"
```

The `settings` parameter allows you to provide alternative regular expressions to capture interpolate, evaluate, and escape snippets. For example, you can replace the evaluate expression from `<% ... %>` to `{{ ... }}` to match the syntax of another templating library called Mustache.js.

Using Underscore templates allows us to create a better solution for the previous subsection example. We have created a new web page `index-templates-js.html` and a new JavaScript file `index-templates-js.js` that use `_.template()`. Here is the code from `index-templates-js.js` that handles the last two button click events from `index-templates-js.html` and renders the same template in two different contexts:

```
var clientsTemplate = _.template(
  "<ul><li>" +
  "<%_.forEach(clients, function (client,index) {%>" +
  "<%if (index>0) {%>" +
  "</li><li>" +
  "<%}%>" +
  "<%=transformations.getContactNameIdAndType(client)%>" +
  "<%})%>" +
  "</li></ul>");
$("#oldest-clients-btn").click(function() {
  $(".panel-heading").html("Top 5 oldest clients with name, id
  and type");
  var displayContent = clientsTemplate({
    clients: oldestClients
  });
});
```

```
$(".panel-body").html(
  displayContent);
});
$("#best-clients-btn").click(function() {
  $(".panel-heading").html("Top 5 best clients with name, id and
  type");
  var displayContent = clientsTemplate({
    clients: bestClients
  });
  $(".panel-body").html(
    displayContent);
});
```

The highlighted code demonstrates that Underscore template interpolation works for function calls and not only for variables. This feature makes Underscore a simple yet very powerful templating solution. You can find this example in the same folder `browser-underscore` from the source code for this chapter.

When dealing with larger templates, you might find the process of building Underscore templates from JavaScript strings a bit unwieldy. An alternative is to embed the template in a `script` element on the web page and pass its contents to the `_.template()` function. In the `index-templates-html.html` file, there is a new script element that replaces the previous example template:

```
<script type="text/template" id="clients-template">
  <ul>
    <li>
      <%_.forEach(clients, function (client,index) {%>
        <%if (index>0) {%>
    </li>
    <li>
      <%}%>
        <%=transformations.getContactNameIdAndType(client)%>
          <%})%>
    </li>
  </ul>
</script>
```

We can now get load the template contents in `index-templates-html.js` using jQuery:

```
var clientsTemplate = _.template($("#clients-template").html());
```

It is worth mentioning that using templates in Underscore is a two-phase process. First, the _.template() call compiles the HTML snippet received as input and returns a function that can be reused as many times as needed. Second, the returned function is invoked with a specific data input and generates the rendered output. The first phase is usually more computationally expensive than the second, hence the benefit of using templates compared to regular string operations. As a general rule templates should contain as little logic as possible to make them more readable and easier to test.

The rest of the code is unchanged from the previous example, and you can find all the files in the same folder browser-underscore from the source code for this chapter.

As mentioned before, Underscore was initially extracted from a project that also used another client-side framework created by the same author called Backbone.js. Backbone is a JavaScript **Model-View-Controller (MVC)** framework that depends on Underscore and uses it to power a lot of the framework functionality, including the default templating system. You can find more about Backbone at http://backbonejs. org/ and in the excellent free-to-read online book *Developing Backbone.js Applications, Addy Osmani, O'Reilly* available at http://addyosmani. github.io/backbone-fundamentals/.

Using Underscore on the server with Node.js

In *Chapter 1, Getting Started with Underscore.js*, we briefly introduced Node.js together with instructions on how to install and use its package manager npm. By using Node.js from the operating system command line, we can execute JavaScript server-side code: JavaScript runs inside the Node.js process with full access to operating system resources.

Executing JavaScript with Node.js

At this point, Node.js and npm are available in the command line, and if we execute the command node, you should see a prompt > appearing in the console waiting for further input. We have launched Node.js as an interactive shell, which is similar to the browser JavaScript console mode, and we can now execute any JavaScript code and immediately see the feedback in the console. We can create a new object, read one of its properties, and then add a new property and read the new property all in the same interactive shell session (I used the Mac OS X terminal for this example):

```
MacBook-Air:~ alex$ node
> var item1 = {id: 1, name: "Item1"};
```

```
undefined
> item1.name
'Item1'
> item1.isProcessed = true;
true
> item1.isProcessed
true
```

Each command has some type of feedback in the interactive shell, and this mode of operation is known as **read-eval-print loop** or **REPL** (you should already be familiar with it if you used the browser JavaScript console). You can exit the REPL at anytime by pressing *Ctrl + C* and resume normal command-line operations.

Node.js can also execute a JavaScript program file if specified in the command line. We will rewrite the previous example as an index.js file with the following content:

```
var item1 = {
  id: 1,
  name: "Item 1"
};
console.log("item1.name: " + item1.name);
item1.isProcessed = true;
console.log("item1.isProcessed: " + item1.isProcessed);
```

Notice that we have not used the revealing module pattern here to isolate scope, and we don't need to as in Node.js global scope is not the default execution scope. Only when we execute Node.js in REPL mode does the global scope behave in a similar manner to the browser and becomes the default scope. Also, in the browser the variable window holds the reference to the global scope, while in Node.js global scope is referenced by the global variable and both objects are different in structure. Only in the Node.js REPL mode does the this variable references the global scope and returns the global object.

The "use strict;" line used in our previous JavaScript examples is also missing because Node.js supports a global command-line switch that enables the ES5 strict mode for any code executed in the current process. The code snippet is using console.log() to output text in the console and this functionality is similar to the browser JavaScript console. We will run the next command line and Node.js will execute the index.js file in the ES5 strict mode:

```
node index.js --use_strict
```

We should see this output in the command-line console; it is similar with the previous example output from the REPL:

```
item1.name: Item 1
item1.isProcessed: true
```

Using Node.js modules

Node.js only accepts one file in its start arguments and relies on its built-in module system to identify and execute code from multiple files.

The previous example used an `index.js` file that is actually loaded by Node.js as a module:

- A Node.js module is a code abstraction used to encapsulate and share JavaScript objects and functions

- Any module has one to one mapping to a file

- A module has a specific syntax to make functions and objects available to other modules through the built-in Node.js expressions `exports` and `module.exports`

- A module can reference other modules through the built-in Node.js `require()` function

To illustrate how modules are declared and used, we will move the code from the previous example into a `module1.js` file and change the `index.js` file to load the `module1.js` file as a module using `require()`. The contents of the `index.js` file are listed next, and we can execute this code by running the same command from the previous example:

```
var module1 = require('./module1.js');
console.log("module1:" + JSON.stringify(module1));
//=> module1:{}
```

We are displaying the object returned by `require()` in the console; in its current form, `module1` does not provide any functionality outside its local scope. A Node.js module has built-in access to a local variable called `module`, which can be used to "export" functionality for other modules. If we add the line `module.exports = item1;` at the end of the `module1.js` file, the console output changes to:

```
module1:{"id":1,"name":"Item 1","isProcessed":true}
```

By using `module.exports`, we can export an object or a function and this gives us full control what is shared with other modules. Node.js also provides a shortcut variable called `exports` that can be used to export multiple objects or functions from the current module. You can find an example of using `exports` in the `module2.js` file that sits together with the updated `index.js` file in the `nodejs-modules` folder, from the source code for this chapter.

Locating modules

In the previous subsection examples, the `require()` function located the target module by using the `./` prefix that made the search relative to the current file `index.js`. You can specify the full path to a file by using the prefix `/` or you can just specify the module name without any path information. The `require()` search algorithm will first check whether the module name matches a built in Node.js module name (as Node.js itself comes with a series of default modules such as `http` or `net`). The next step is to search the requested module within a `node_modules` folder in the current folder, and if the module is not found, then the same search will continue in the parent folder recursively until the top-level folder is reached. This algorithm is used whenever we import modules installed through npm.

The target module can be specified as a folder name or a folder path (absolute or relative), and the `require()` function will first locate the folder, and if the found folder has an `index.js` file, then the module will be loaded from this file. You can find an example in the `nodejs-modules/shared/module3` folder from the source code for this chapter. This module is loaded by relative path in the `nodejs-modules/index.js` file:

```
var module3 = require('./shared/module3');
```

If the target module is in a folder that has a `package.json` file, this file will be used to locate the module file. You can find an example (in the `nodejs-modules/shared/module4` folder from the source code for this chapter) that has a `package.json` file and a folder `src` with a `namedModule.js` file inside it. The contents of the `package.json` file are displayed next with the module file location specified in the `main` property:

```
{
  "name": "module4",
  "main": "./src/namedModule.js"
}
```

Loading `module4` is very similar with loading `module3`, while their folder structure is very different and you can find the matching `require()` call in the `nodejs-modules/index.js` file.

> Node.js module files can be specified without any extension and the `require()` function will append `.js`, `.json`, and `.node` extensions to locate its target. You can find more about these types of files and modules in general in the official documentation at `https://nodejs.org/api/modules.html`.

Creating a npm package

We will now proceed to convert the example found in the folder `browser-underscore` to its Node.js equivalent. The first step is to create a copy in the `nodejs-underscore` folder and then remove all files required for rendering the example in a browser: the `bower_components` folder, `bower.json`, and all `.html` files. We will only keep the `index-templates-html.js` out of the `index-*.js` files and rename it to `index.js`. We have now created the seed for our Node.js example, and we will integrate it with the npm package manager.

We already established that Node.js associates a single file with a module. Because we have multiple JavaScript files in our `nodejs-underscore` folder, it is a good practice to use a `package.json` file to establish the main module for our example folder. In the previous subsection, we used the `package.json` file to identify the name and the main file for a module, so it can be located by the Node.js runtime. The npm package manager supports additional fields for the `package.json` file and some of them facilitate package maintenance among other features. There are two key fields that we will use to manage dependencies to other npm packages or to packages located outside the npm online repository:

- `dependencies`: This lists other packages that the current package depends on for execution
- `devDependencies`: This lists other packages that the current package depends on for building documentation, running tests, or any other task that is not essential for actually executing the current package

> The npm package manager usually works with its associated online package repository hosted at `https://www.npmjs.com/`. Npm also supports package references that are local packages, Git URLs, or tarball URLs, and you can find more information about the full extent of `package.json` features for npm at `https://docs.npmjs.com/files/package.json`.

We will use the `package.json` file to define the main file for our example folder and to define the dependencies on other packages. To convert our example folder into an npm-compatible package, we need to execute the following command line in the example folder `nodejs-underscore`:

npm init

This command initiates a console-based dialog, and we will accept all incoming prompts with the default values by pressing *Enter* until the dialog is finished.

Next, we will use npm to download the Underscore package and save it as a dependency of our current package by executing the following command-line entry:

npm install underscore --save

We will notice that the `node_modules` folder is created in our example folder with a subdirectory called `underscore`. The current contents of our `package.json` file created by the previous commands are listed in the following code:

```
{
  "name": "nodejs-underscore",
  "version": "1.0.0",
  "description": "",
  "main": "index.js",
  "scripts": {
    "test": "echo \"Error: no test specified\" && exit 1"
  },
  "author": "",
  "license": "ISC",
  "dependencies": {
    "underscore": "^1.8.3"
  }
}
```

We have created an npm-compatible package from our example folder that can be published and distributed through the npm package repository with some minor additional changes. When working with source control repositories, it is a good practice to omit the `node_modules` folders from being committed. We can restore the packages defined in the `package.json` file by running the following command line:

npm install

Converting JavaScript code to Node.js modules

We will now proceed to convert our existing JavaScript files from the `nodejs-underscore` example folder. Most of the changes required are minimal and they mainly consist in removing the redundant code that enforces the revealing module pattern and defining the functions and objects that are exported by the module.

We will start with the `transformations.js` and `validations.js` files. The first file is the simplest, and we will use the `exports` variable for a final output that looks like:

```
exports.getContactNameIdAndType = function(contact) {
  return contact.name + " (" + contact.id + " - " + contact.type +
")";
};
```

Notice how the revealing module pattern-specific code is gone, and we will see a similar change in the `validations.js` file. The code from this file is using Underscore, and we need to explicitly declare this dependency in the following line:

```
var _ = require("underscore");
```

Underscore is configured as an npm dependency, and we can use its module name rather than its path to identify it (Node.js will search by this module name in the `node_modules` folder). The `validations.js` file defines multiple functions that reference each other, and rather than using `exports` as with the previous file, we will use `module.exports` to export the object that contains all the self-referencing functions:

```
var validations = {
  validateArgsLength: function(argsLength, argsArray) {
    ...
  },
  ...
  validateClientArgs: function(argsArray) {
    ...
};
module.exports = validations;
```

The `validations` variable is in effect the object returned by the previous revealing module pattern implementation, and there is no change between the contents of the two objects.

We will explore in *Chapter 7, Underscore.js Build Automation and Code Reusability,* various techniques to share code between client and server environments, and you will see a similar refactoring technique.

The next change is for the `classes.js` file that contains the class definitions, and we will split them in two files `contact.js` and `client.js` so that we can define two separate modules for the two separate classes. The `Contact` class is using both Underscore and functions from the `validations.js` file. We can use `require()` for both dependencies and the final code has minimal changes that are highlighted for clarity:

```
var _ = require("underscore");
var validations = require("./validations");
function Contact(id, name, gender, company, email, phone, address) {
    ...
}
module.exports = Contact;
```

The object constructor function is the only thing exported by the module and similar minimal changes were done for the `Client` class (also highlighted for clarity):

```
var _ = require("underscore");
var Contact = require("./contact");
var validations = require("./validations");
function Client(id, name, gender, company, email, phone, address,
registered, preferredBike, bikePoints, notes) {
    ...
}
Client.prototype = Object.create(Contact.prototype);
Client.prototype.constructor = Client;
module.exports = Client;
```

The `dataProvider.js` and `clientRetriever.js` files are the next ones to be changed, and they follow a similar approach with the `transformations.js` file by using the `exports` variable.

The final changes are done in the `index.js` file where we ensure the relevant `require()` calls are in place, and we replace the code that rendered output to the browser with code that generates output to the console:

```
var _ = require("underscore");
var clientRetriever = require("./clientRetriever");
```

```javascript
var transformations = require("./transformations");

var oldestClients = clientRetriever.getOldestClients(5);
var bestClients = clientRetriever.getBestClients(5);
var clients = clientRetriever.getClients();
console.log("There are " + clients.length + " clients.");
var getContactsOutput = function(clients) {
  var outputText = "";
  _.forEach(clients, function(client, index) {
    if (index > 0) {
      outputText += ", ";
    }
    outputText += transformations.getContactNameIdAndType(client);
  });
  return outputText;
};
console.log("Top 5 oldest clients with name, id and type: " +
getContactsOutput(oldestClients));
console.log("Top 5 best clients with name, id and type: " +
getContactsOutput(bestClients));
```

We also removed the jQuery-specific function $(document).ready() as it is not valid in the Node.js environment. We can now execute the following command line in the example folder to see the previous browser-rendered content being displayed instead in the console:

node index.js --use_strict

Running tests with Node.js

Up until now, we executed tests using the Jasmine test library (installed through the Bower package manager) and by browsing a page such as the SpecRunner.html from the browser-underscore example folder that has references to all the tests files. The Jasmine library also has an npm package that can be used to test Node.js code, and we will install it in our example folder using the following command:

npm install --save-dev jasmine

Notice the --save-dev command-line switch that configures Jasmine as a development dependency, and this means that the package is not required to be included in a production deployment package (it will be saved in the devDependecies entry of the package.json file from the example folder). By installing the Jasmine npm package, we now have access to the Jasmine command-line interface (CLI) executable at the node_modules/.bin/jasmine location.

Using the Jasmine CLI, we can set up the test folder structure for the example folder by executing the next command:

```
node_modules/.bin/jasmine init
```

This command creates a `spec/support/jasmine.json` file with the following content:

```
{
  "spec_dir": "spec",
  "spec_files": [
    "**/*[sS]pec.js"
  ],
  "helpers": [
    "helpers/**/*.js"
  ]
}
```

The JSON file specifies the folder that contains tests in the `spec_dir` entry and the search pattern to find test files in the `spec_files` entry. If we go back and look again at the test files from the `browser-underscore` example folder (or any test files from the book examples), we notice that they already conform to the default `jasmine.json` values. We can copy all the test files from the `browser-underscore/spec` folder to the `nodejs-underscore/spec` folder and execute the Jasmine CLI to run the tests with the command:

```
node_modules/.bin/jasmine
```

Although all test specifications are discovered and executed by Jasmine, they will all fail as code under test needs to be initialized explicitly as Node.js modules. It is just a matter of ensuring that all test specifications include a module import for all the modules they depend on like the next one found in the `spec/ContactSpec.js` file:

```
var Contact = require("../contact");
```

If we execute the tests again, we should see that they all pass now.

Using Underscore with MongoDB

In the last decade, we have seen a wide range of successful alternatives to relational databases becoming more and more popular. These alternative databases are usually referred to as NoSQL databases and their common denominator should be read as an abbreviation for "not only SQL". Among such databases that specialize in big data analysis such as Hadoop or that specialize in key-value storage such as Redis, there is MongoDB (with the name derived from "humongous")—a popular document database that recently reached version 3.

MongoDB like other similar document database engines stores data in databases that contain collections of documents:

- A document is a set of keys and values (or fields) that can be expressed in JSON format and it is stored internally as BSON (binary JSON — a more efficient JSON-derived format). A document can contain other nested documents, and you can visualize it as a JavaScript object literal.

- A collection is simply a container of documents and it does not enforce any specific document structure. The documents stored in a collection can differ significantly in their structure (they are **schema-less**), but they will always have at least one _id field with a unique value throughout the document collection.

We can draw a parallel with relational databases:

- A collection is similar to a table that does not have any structure
- A document can be seen as a row that has a variable number of fields
- The _id field of a document is like the primary key of a table

MongoDB and Node.js can be a great match when used together:

- MongoDB uses a built-in JavaScript V8 engine similar with Node.js.
- The MongoDB database shell is using JavaScript to execute data commands or queries and to define more advanced database operations. It can be configured using JavaScript files, it can execute JavaScript files, and it can load other JavaScript files.
- Node.js is officially supported by the MongoDB database through an npm package called mongodb that contains a native database driver implementation.

We will explore the relationship between MongoDB, Node.js, and Underscore by converting the example from the previous section to use MongoDB for data storage. We will then use the MongoDB database shell to create the initial data in a database, and we will extract data from the database with the Node.js driver. We will only cover features of MongoDB that are used in the examples so a lot of the functionality around security, replication, sharding, and administration will be left out.

MongoDB has its own excellent free online and offline documentation in the form of the MongoDB Manual available at https://docs.mongodb.org/manual/. I recommend reading the *Getting Started* section. There is another free online MongoDB book called *The Little MongoDB Book, Karl Seguin,* available at http://openmymind.net/2011/3/28/The-Little-MongoDB-Book/ that is a great and quick way of getting familiar with MongoDB.

Installing and configuring MongoDB

First of all, we need to install the MongoDB database from its official download address at `http://www.mongodb.org/downloads`.

Installing MongoDB on Windows

For Windows systems, we will use the 64-bit version and install it with the default options. The default options will install MongoDB in the `C:\mongodb` folder. In the MongoDB installation folder, you will find a `bin` folder that contains the main executables: `mongod.exe` that runs the database engine and `mongo.exe` that starts the database shell (also referred to as the MongoDB client). MongoDB assumes another default path for the local databases at `C:\data\db` (for which it should have read and write permissions) and, when we execute `mongod.exe`, it will try and load all databases found at this path. You can find more information about installing MongoDB on Windows at `https://docs.mongodb.org/manual/tutorial/install-mongodb-on-windows/`.

Installing MongoDB on Ubuntu Linux

MongoDB is included in the default Ubuntu Linux software package and to install it you need to execute the following command line:

```
sudo apt-get install -y mongodb
```

To start and stop the `mongod` process, you need to execute the following commands:

```
sudo service mongod start
sudo service mongod stop
```

If you prefer to use the packages provided directly by the MongoDB team, you can follow the instructions available at `https://docs.mongodb.org/manual/administration/install-on-linux/`.

Installing MongoDB on Mac OS X

Installing MongoDB on Mac OS X is a very quick task when using the Homebrew package manager (see `http://brew.sh/` for Homebrew installation instructions). If case, this is not installed on your system and you don't want to give it a try you can download the 64-bit MongoDB binaries for Mac OS X from `http://www.mongodb.org/downloads` and follow the instructions at `https://docs.mongodb.org/manual/tutorial/install-mongodb-on-os-x/`. We assume you have Homebrew available, and in this case you just need to execute the following command line to install MongoDB and add its executables to the `PATH` variable:

```
brew install mongodb
```

The only additional step is to create the /data/db folder and give read and write permissions for the currently logged on user.

Configuring and running MongoDB

In the rest of the section, we assume that both the mongod and mongo processes are added to your specific environment PATH variable, and if this is not the case we assume you know how to invoke them using their full path, for example, C:\ mongodb\bin\mongod and C:\mongodb\bin\mongo (for Windows systems). If you prefer a different location for your database files, the mongod process can take a different default database path via the command line or in the MongoDB configuration file mongodb.config and you can find more details about how to configure MongoDB at https://docs.mongodb.org/manual/tutorial/manage-mongodb-processes/. To execute the examples from this section, you need to ensure the mongod process is running successfully in the background first by using the MongoDB start command line specific to your environment.

Creating initial data using the MongoDB client and Underscore

We will use the MongoDB database shell (also known as the MongoDB client) by launching the mongo executable. The MongoDB client will connect to the local MongoDB database instance using address 127.0.0.1 and port 27017, and then it will start the MongoDB database prompt. You can then execute MongoDB database commands and the MongoDB client supports:

- Database shell helper commands that are similar with other relational database commands such as: show dbs (displays a list of existing databases), use <db> (selects <db> as the current database), and show collections (displays a list of collections for the current database)

- Database shell commands that use the MongoDB JavaScript API such as: db.adminCommand('listDatabases') (displays a list of existing databases), db = db.getSiblingDB('<db>') (selects <db> as the current database), and db.getCollectionNames() (displays a list of collections for the current database)

In this section, we will use the MongoDB JavaScript API because we can save a MongoDB client script as a JavaScript file and use the mongo executable to run the JavaScript file directly in unattended mode. The client helper commands are available only when we launch the mongo executable in interactive mode.

You can find more details about the full MongoDB client scripting capabilities at `https://docs.mongodb.org/manual/administration/scripting/`.

We will start by launching the MongoDB client and passing an argument to a JavaScript file that displays information about the current database and its collections. You can select a database even if it is not created and you can also access its collections. I have prepared a script that sets the current database to be `underscorejs-examples` and then it enumerates the database object properties using both Underscore and a built in MongoDB console output function. These are the contents of the `data\ getDatabaseInfo.js` file located in the `mongodb-underscore` folder from the source code for this chapter:

```
db = db.getSiblingDB('underscorejs-examples');
print("Current database is set to: " + tojson(db));
load("node_modules/underscore/underscore.js");

print("Showing current database properties using Underscore: ");
_.each(db, function(value, key) {
  print("key: " + key + ", value: " + value);
});
print("Showing current database properties using tojson(): " +
tojson(db));

var collectionNames = db.getCollectionNames();
print('Collection list: ' + tojson(collectionNames));

_.each(collectionNames, function(collectionName) {
  print("Collection " + collectionName + " has " +
  db.getCollection(collectionName).count() + " documents.");
});
```

The first line selects the current database and the second one displays information about the database object using the MongoDB built in functions `print()` and `tojson()`. These functions are similar with `console.log()` and `JSON.stringify()` available in the browser and Node.js environments. The MongoDB V8 JavaScript engine is fully compliant with ECMAScript 5 and it also supports `JSON. stringify()`.

The MongoDB client can load other JavaScript files by using their absolute or relative path using the built in `load()` function. Any variable or function that is defined in the loaded JavaScript file becomes available for use by the MongoDB client. The highlighted code snippet shows how we load the Underscore library from its npm local package and use its _ variable to display the enumerable properties of the current database in the command line console. We also use `JSON.stringify()` to display the JSON version of the current database object. The last section of the script enumerates the database collections and displays their document count.

We will execute the `data\getDatabaseInfo.js` file using the MongoDB client by typing the following command line from the `mongodb-underscore` folder:

```
mongo data/getDatabaseInfo.js
```

You should see this output:

```
MongoDB shell version: 3.0.1
connecting to: test
Current database is set to: underscorejs-examples
Showing enumerable database properties using Underscore:
key: _mongo, value: connection to 127.0.0.1
key: _name, value: underscorejs-examples
Showing all database properties using JSON.stringify(): {"_mongo":{"slave
Ok":false,"host":"127.0.0.1"},"_name":"underscorejs-examples","_defaultAu
thenticationMechanism":null,"_defaultGssapiServiceName":"mongodb"}
Collection list: [ ]
```

Inserting MongoDB documents into a collection is an extremely simple process with the `db.collection.insert(data)` function where `data` can be an object or an array of objects. If the objects about to be inserted don't have an `_id` field, MongoDB will set it to an auto-generated value of type `ObjectId`—a 12-byte BSON type composed from a 4-byte timestamp, a 3-byte machine identifier, a 2-byte process ID, and a 3-byte counter based on a random seed. This value can be used to calculate the creation time of the document and can be used to sort documents by creation time.

> The `db.collections.insert()` function accepts a second parameter that can specify the insert order or change how the insert operation is done. You can find more information at `https://docs.mongodb.org/manual/reference/method/db.collection.insert/#db.collection.insert`.

If you insert two documents with the same _id field value, the last inserted document will overwrite the previously inserted one. The example script that will be used to insert documents will check whether the target collection is empty beforehand.

We will now move the functions that generate the initial data sample from the dataProvider.js file into the data\insertSeedData.js file that can be found in the mongodb-underscore folder from the source code for this chapter. The first change is to rename all id fields to _id to ensure they become MongoDB primary key values when persisted to the database. We will then create the actual insert script at data\insertSeedData.js with the following contents:

```
db = db.getSiblingDB('underscorejs-examples');
print("Current database is set to: " + tojson(db));
load("data/generateSeedData.js");
if (db.bicycles.count() === 0) {
  var bicycles = getBicycles();
  print("Inserting " + bicycles.length + " bicycles ...");
  var result = db.bicycles.insert(bicycles);
  printjson(result);
} else {
  print("The bicycles collection is not empty. Skipping seed data
  insertion for bicycles.");
}
if (db.clients.count() === 0) {
  var clients = getClients();
  print("Inserting " + clients.length + " clients ...");
  var result = db.clients.insert(clients);
  printjson(result);
} else {
  print("The clients collection is not empty. Skipping seed data
  insertion for clients.");
}
if (db.clientOrders.count() === 0) {
  var clientOrders = getClientOrders();
  print("Inserting " + clientOrders.length + " client orders ...");
  var result = db.clientOrders.insert(clientOrders);
  printjson(result);
} else {
  print("The client orders collection is not empty. Skipping seed
  data insertion for client orders.");
}
```

The highlighted code snippet shows how the data generation functions are loaded in the MongoDB client and then used to get the array of documents about to be inserted. The db.collection.insert() function returns a WriteResult object when a single document is inserted or a BulkWriteResult object when an array of documents is inserted. The console output for the highlighted code is:

```
Inserting 12 bicycles ...
{
    "writeErrors" : [ ],
    "writeConcernErrors" : [ ],
    "nInserted" : 12,
    "nUpserted" : 0,
    "nMatched" : 0,
    "nModified" : 0,
    "nRemoved" : 0,
    "upserted" : [ ]
}
```

To see the example output you need to run this command line:

```
mongo data/insertSeedData.js
```

We can also inspect the database collections again using the command line:

```
mongo data/getDatabaseInfo.js
```

The console output for collections is now different:

```
Collection list: [ "bicycles", "clientOrders", "clients", "system.
indexes" ]
Collection bicycles has 12 documents.
Collection clientOrders has 250 documents.
Collection clients has 250 documents.
Collection system.indexes has 3 documents.
```

Notice that we have an additional collection system.indexes that was automatically created by MongoDB to store the indexes created for the collections primary keys—the _id fields. For convenience, I also created a script data/dropDatabase.js to delete the sample database so you can run the examples repeatedly.

Asynchronous programming in Node.js

Up until now, all the Node.js code that we used has been synchronous: all the functions that we implemented returned the results immediately. When working with databases, you will always have an amount of latency involved, due to the cost of retrieving the data or due to network throughput when working with a remote database. And this is where using the Node.js asynchronous (or non-blocking) API stops database latencies from affecting the overall throughput of the application. Node.js uses by design a single thread of execution to avoid the complexity of multithreaded runtimes. To counter the lack of multithreading, any input/output (I/O) computer operation such as a database call, a file system task, or a remote API request does not block the Node.js execution thread.

The following example shows a synchronous function call that will be used for comparison with an equivalent asynchronous version:

```
var outputValue = syncFunction(inputValue);
processOutput(outputValue);
```

The asynchronous (or non-blocking) version has different signature:

```
asyncFunction(inputValue, function(outputValue) {
  processResult(outputValue);
});
```

The second parameter is a callback function that will be invoked only when `asyncFunction` finishes processing and can return a result. If the processing happens as part of an I/O operation the Node.js execution thread will continue unaffected. This is an event-driven programming model that ensures a high throughput.

> The powerful npm module async can help with simplifying asynchronous code by providing many built in helper functions. You can find more details at `https://www.npmjs.com/package/async`.

Accessing data using the MongoDB Node.js driver

At this point, we should have data available in the MongoDB database, and we will use Node.js to access it by modifying `dataProvider.js` to extract data using the MongoDB driver. First, we will install the MongoDB Node.js driver as a dependency in the `package.json` file using the following command line:

```
npm install mongodb --save
```

The MongoDB driver is similar to the MongoDB JavaScript API while being a Node.js idiomatic implementation. The driver API is asynchronous and it is relying on callback functions to return its results for further processing. This ensures all I/O operations are non-blocking, leaving the Node.js execution thread to process other requests.

The module implemented in the `dataProvider.js` file will open the local MongoDB database connection, extract the data requested, and then close the database connection after the data request is finished. The following example shows the asynchronous version of the `getBicycles()` call:

```
var MongoClient = require('mongodb').MongoClient
var dbUrl = 'mongodb://localhost:27017/underscorejs-examples';
var getBicycles = function(callback) {
  MongoClient.connect(dbUrl, function(err, db) {
    var collection = db.collection('bicycles');
    collection.find({}).toArray(function(err, bicycles) {
      callback(bicycles);
      db.close();
    });
  });
};
```

First of all, we referenced the MongoDB client object and we stored the MongoDB database address to the previously created instance. After connecting to the MongoDB database using the `connect()` function, we selected the target collection `bicycles` and extracted all documents using the `collection.find()` function. The `collection.find()` function accepts as its first argument an object that will be used to filter the results and returns a `Cursor` object that can return data sequentially by calling `Cursor.next()`. In this example, we used `Cursor.toArray()` to return all the documents at once and we have not filtered the results.

The highlighted MongoDB API calls are asynchronous and they expect a callback function to be provided for delivering their results. The `callback` variable stores the function that will be called after the database call has ended and will receive the database call result as an argument.

 You can see another functional technique at play, as `getBicycles()` is a function that accepts another function as an argument. This is a good technique to use when working with asynchronous APIs to avoid nested callbacks and make debugging and troubleshooting easier.

You can find similar implementations for the `getClients()` and `getClientOrders()` functions in the same file.

As we introduced asynchronous functions in the `dataProvider` module used in `clientRetriever.js` and `index.js`, we now need to propagate the asynchronous calls up the chain. This is how the `clientRetriever.getContacts()` looks after the change:

```
var getContacts = function(callback) {
  dataProvider.getClients(function(clientObjects) {
    var contacts = _.map(clientObjects, function(clientObject) {
      if (!clientObject.isActive) {
        return new Contact(
          clientObject._id,
          clientObject.name,
          clientObject.gender,
          clientObject.company,
          clientObject.email,
          clientObject.phone,
          clientObject.address);
      }
      return new Client(
        clientObject._id,
        clientObject.name,
        clientObject.gender,
        clientObject.company,
        clientObject.email,
        clientObject.phone,
        clientObject.address,
        new Date(clientObject.registered),
        clientObject.preferredBike,
        clientObject.bikePoints,
        clientObject.notes
      );
    });
    callback(contacts);
  });
};
```

The function takes a `callback` argument that will be invoked after the data is retrieved from the database and converted to class instances. Further up the chain, the `index.js` code needs to be changed to an asynchronous version:

```
clientRetriever.getClients(function(clients) {
  console.log("There are " + clients.length + " clients.");
});
```

You can find the other changed functions in the `mongodb-underscore` folder from the source code for this chapter.

 In this section, we only scratched the surface of the MongoDB Node.js driver functionality. You can find more information on how to use the MongoDB Node.js driver at `http://mongodb.github.io/node-mongodb-native/2.0/`.

Using Underscore with PostgreSQL

In this section, we will introduce PostgreSQL, which is a mature relational database engine that started as a research project at University of California in mid-1980s and surfaced as a community open source project with a permissive license (similar with a BSD license) in 1995.

In 2014, PostgreSQL 9.4 was released and introduced a new binary JSON (JSONB) data type support alongside its existing JSON data type support. This allows for more efficient storage and for better performance through JSONB indexing capabilities.

Another feature that makes it interesting for us is that it supports JavaScript as a procedural language through the PL/v8 project. A procedural language can be used to create user-defined functions and PostgreSQL alongside SQL and C has built-in support for procedural languages such as Python, Perl, and Tcl through PL/Python, PL/Perl, and PL/Tcl. Many other procedural languages are supported through community contributions and PL/v8 is one of them, using the same JavaScript V8 engine that powers Google Chrome, Node.js, and MongoDB.

SQL support in PostgreSQL is very solid and comparable with commercial database engines such as Microsoft SQL Server and Oracle (in features, reliability, and performance), and we will not explore it here. Apart from installation and configuration topics, we will only discuss the JSONB data type and the PL/v8 procedural language that makes it an attractive alternative for document databases such as MongoDB.

 PostgreSQL has more than 2,500 pages in its community-supported manual available at `http://www.postgresql.org/docs/9.4/static/index.html`. I recommend reading the `http://www.postgresql.org/docs/9.4/static/tutorial.html` topics for an excellent general introduction to this database.

Installing and configuring PostgreSQL

PostgreSQL supports a large number of operating systems and it comes installed by default on many of them. You can find installers and detailed instructions at `http://www.postgresql.org/download/`. We will need the PostgreSQL 9.4 version for this section. The PL/v8 procedural language is provided through the plv8 project binaries (`https://github.com/plv8/plv8`) that are installed differently depending on your environment.

Once installed and with the database engine running, the main way to interact with the PostgreSQL database engine is through the psql executable that provides a command-line interface similar with other database engines, for example, mssql for Microsoft SQL Server or sqlplus for Oracle.

 PostgreSQL has a series of GUI clients such as pgAdmin that you can be used as an alternative to psql. The Windows installer includes pgAdmin by default and you can install the Mac OS X version from here `http://www.pgadmin.org/download/macosx.php`. On Ubuntu, pgAdmin can be installed by following the instructions at `https://help.ubuntu.com/community/PostgreSQL`.

Installing PostgreSQL on Windows

Download and install the package for PostgreSQL from `http://www.postgresql.org/download/windows/`. As part of the installation, the database administrator user `postgres` is created and you need to set its password. After installation, you need to retrieve the plv8 binaries from `http://bit.ly/1Q5iLMC` and copy them to your PostgreSQL installation folder (usually `C:\Program Files\PostgreSQL\9.4` or see the `README.txt` file for more details).

You can then launch psql via the **PostgreSQL 9.4 | SQL Shell (psql)** link from the Windows Start menu's **All Programs** folder. At that point, you need to authenticate using the `postgres` user and the password you created earlier and after that you should have initiated successfully the `psql` session.

Installing PostgreSQL on Ubuntu Linux

PostgreSQL 9.4 is available on Ubuntu 14.10 or greater and you can install it using the following command line:

```
sudo apt-get install postgresql-9.4
```

If you are on an earlier Ubuntu version you need to enable the official package repositories by following the instructions from `https://wiki.postgresql.org/wiki/Apt`. On the same page, you can find the link `http://bit.ly/1Otwuci` for a shell script that will perform this change for you. Assuming you downloaded it to your home directory, you can run the following command line using the friendly name of your Ubuntu release at the end, for example, `trusty` for Ubuntu 14.04:

```
sudo bash ./apt.postgresql.org.sh trusty
```

After this step, you can install PostgreSQL 9.4 using the official PostgreSQL repository.

The plv8 package needs to be installed next through the command line:

```
sudo apt-get install postgresql-9.4-plv8
```

You can then connect to the local PostgreSQL instance using the database administration user `postgres` with the next command line:

```
sudo -u postgres psql postgres
```

The psql session is now started and you need to set the password for the `postgresql` user before any database command can be executed. The following psql command line will start the password change task:

```
\password postgres
```

Installing PostgreSQL on Mac OS X

The Mac OS X version can be installed in many different ways as detailed at `http://www.postgresql.org/download/macosx/`. For Mac OS X, we have the most convenient and simple way to install PostgreSQL through the PostgreSQL.app from `http://postgresapp.com/`. This easily installable package also includes the plv8 binaries, so I strongly recommend it. After installation, start the PostgreSQL. app application, and the database engine will create a database using your current username on its first launch. To initiate the psql session, you need to click the **Open psql** link from the application screen or from the application tray icon menu.

Using psql with basic database commands

With the psql interactive session started, you can now launch database commands against the local PostgreSQL database. Apart from the SQL command psql has a series of internal command that can be executed using a \ prefix.

The following psql commands will list the current database, create a new database, and select the newly created database (`\c` is a shortcut for `\connect`):

```
\l
CREATE DATABASE underscorejs_examples;
\c underscorejs_examples
```

The second line is a SQL command while the first and last are internal psql commands. The third command should be executed before any other example when running psql in interactive mode to ensure the changes only affect this specific database. The current database can also be specified as a psql argument with the `-d` switch. After the current database is selected your psql command prompt should change to `underscorejs_examples=#`.

The psql session can execute commands using the underlying OS command prompt when the commands are prefixed with `\!`. The following psql commands will display the current working directory and the first one is for Linux/Mac OS X with the second one for Windows:

```
\! pwd
\! echo %cd%
```

We will now proceed to set the psql working directory to your local copy of the `postgresql-underscore` from the source code for this chapter. We will use the `\cd` internal psql command and this is what I had to run on a Linux/Mac OS X environment:

```
\cd '/Users/alex/Documents/underscorejs-examples/browser-server-database/
postgresql-underscore'
```

Notice the enclosing single quotes that need to surround the target path. For the rest of the section, we assume that:

- Your PostgreSQL database engine is running and it is configured correctly
- You have a psql command prompt open and connected to the `underscorejs_examples` database
- Your psql command prompt has its working directory set to your local copy of the `postgresql-underscore` folder from the source code for this chapter

PostgreSQL data types

PostgreSQL like similar relational database engines has extensive support for SQL data types, including numeric, character, binary, date/time, boolean, and composite types (known in other database engines as user-defined types). It also has support for specialized types such as monetary, enumerated, geometric, network address types, text search, JSON types, and even arrays to name just some of them. You can find more information about all supported types at `http://www.postgresql.org/docs/9.4/static/datatype.html`.

SQL types

To show some of the PostgreSQL types, we will create a table to store the bicycle objects used in the previous examples, insert a couple of rows, and then view the inserted rows:

```
CREATE TABLE bicycles_sql(
    id serial primary key,
    name text not null,
    type varchar(255) not null,
    quantity smallint,
    rent_price numeric,
    date_added timestamp
);
INSERT INTO bicycles_sql (name, type, quantity, rent_price, date_
added)
VALUES
    ('A fast bike', 'Road Bike', 10, 20,'2015-02-02'),
    ('An even faster bike', 'Road Bike', 4, 25, '2015-03-25'),
    ('A springy bike', 'Mountain Bike', 20, 18, '2014-11-01');
SELECT * FROM bicycles_sql;
DROP TABLE bicycles_sql;
```

The output in the psql console should look like this:

```
CREATE TABLE
INSERT 0 3
 id |        name         |     type      | quantity | rent_price |     date_added
----+---------------------+---------------+----------+------------+---------------------
  1 | A fast bike         | Road Bike     |       10 |         20 | 2015-02-02 00:00:00
  2 | An even faster bike | Road Bike     |        4 |         25 | 2015-03-25 00:00:00
  3 | A springy bike      | Mountain Bike |       20 |         18 | 2014-11-01 00:00:00
(3 rows)
```

The code should look familiar if you have used a relational database before as PostgreSQL closely follows the SQL standards. The database object names are case-sensitive and we used a typical naming style. The first table column id is of the type serial, which is an auto-incremented integer. The numeric type for the rent_price column is a decimal type (it can also be aliased as decimal) and the date_added column timestamp type stores date and time values without time zone information. You can find the example in the bicyclesTable_SQL.sql file in the postgresql-underscore folder from the source code for this chapter.

The jsonb type

One of the most important features in PostgreSQL 9.4 is the support for the jsonb type. PostgreSQL already supports the json type that stores text that is a valid JSON value. The jsonb type stores JSON as binary data and with the JSON field types mapped to PostgreSQL column types internally. This enables more efficient storage and improved query performance through indexing.

This is how we declare and insert into a table for our bicycle objects using the jsonb type (creating what is effectively a document store):

```
CREATE TABLE bicycles(
    id int primary key,
    body jsonb not null
);
INSERT INTO bicycles (id, body)
VALUES
(1, '{ "id": 1,
      "name": "A fast bike",
      "type": "Road Bike",
      "quantity": 10,
      "rentPrice": 20,
    "dateAdded": "2015-02-02T00:00:00.000Z" }'),
(2, '{ "id": 2,
      "name": "An even faster bike",
      "type": "Road Bike",
      "quantity": 4,
      "rentPrice": 25,
      "dateAdded": "2015-03-25T00:00:00.000Z" }'),
(3, '{ "id": 3,
      "name": "A springy bike",
```

```
            "type": "Mountain Bike",
            "quantity": 20,
            "rentPrice": 18,
            "dateAdded": "2014-11-01T00:00:00.000Z" }');
   SELECT * FROM bicycles;
```

We inserted the JSON values as text and PostgreSQL will internally convert the
JSON field values to existing SQL types such as text, numeric, or boolean (and
(none) for null JSON field values). The output for this query should look like this:

```
 id |                                            body
----+----------------------------------------------------------------------------------------------
  1 | {"id": 1, "name": "A fast bike", "type": "Road Bike", "quantity": 10, "dateAdded": "2015-02-02T00:00:00.000Z", "rentPrice": 20}
  2 | {"id": 2, "name": "An even faster bike", "type": "Road Bike", "quantity": 4, "dateAdded": "2015-03-25T00:00:00.000Z", "rentPrice": 25}
  3 | {"id": 3, "name": "A springy bike", "type": "Mountain Bike", "quantity": 20, "dateAdded": "2014-11-01T00:00:00.000Z", "rentPrice": 18}
(3 rows)
```

Notice how the order of the JSON fields was changed and this shows that the jsonb
type is storing values verbatim and is parsing the input first. A similar query for the
same column using the json type instead of jsonb would show the inserted values
exactly as they were inserted.

The PostgreSQL support for json and jsonb types is extended through specialized
functions that convert table rows to these data types. The reverse operation is also
possible and we will use a function that will convert the jsonb data into rows:

```
   SELECT converted.id, name, type, quantity, "rentPrice","dateAdded"
   FROM bicycles, jsonb_to_record(body) AS
     converted (
       id int,
       name text,
       type varchar(255),
       quantity smallint,
       "rentPrice" numeric,
       "dateAdded" timestamp);
```

The highlighted function transforms the data into a SQL-compatible format bridging
the gap between NoSQL documents and SQL table records. The query output looks
now like a typical SQL table output:

```
 id |         name         |     type      | quantity | rentPrice |      dateAdded
----+----------------------+---------------+----------+-----------+---------------------
  1 | A fast bike          | Road Bike     |       10 |        20 | 2015-02-02 00:00:00
  2 | An even faster bike  | Road Bike     |        4 |        25 | 2015-03-25 00:00:00
  3 | A springy bike       | Mountain Bike |       20 |        18 | 2014-11-01 00:00:00
(3 rows)
```

PostgreSQL also supports JSON field selectors, which are useful when working with complex nested documents. We have rewritten the previous query using JSON selectors getting a similar output:

```
SELECT  body->'id' AS id,
        body->'name' AS name,
        body->'type' AS type,
        (body->>'quantity')::smallint AS quantity,
        body->'rentPrice' AS rent_price,
        (body->>'dateAdded')::timestamp AS date_added
FROM bicycles;
```

The -> selector returns the JSON field as jsonb while the ->> selector returns the JSON fields as text, allowing a conversion to the desired type. You can find the example in the bicyclesTable_JSONB.sql file in the postgresql-underscore folder from the source code for this chapter.

> You can find more information about support for json, jsonb types, and related functions at http://www.postgresql.org/docs/9.4/static/datatype-json.html and at http://www.postgresql.org/docs/9.4/static/functions-json.html.

Using PostgreSQL with plv8

Procedural languages are enabled for each database separately and the next line of SQL will enable the PL/v8 language for the current database:

```
CREATE EXTENSION IF NOT EXISTS plv8;
```

We can now leverage JavaScript as a language and implement PostgreSQL functions or execute ad hoc code. A PostgreSQL function in a specific procedural language is created and invoked like this:

```
CREATE FUNCTION plv8_test(keys text[], vals text[]) RETURNS text AS $$
    var o = {};
    for(var i=0; i<keys.length; i++){
        o[keys[i]] = vals[i];
    }
    return JSON.stringify(o);
$$ LANGUAGE plv8 IMMUTABLE STRICT;
SELECT plv8_test(ARRAY['name', 'age'], ARRAY['Alex', '37']);
```

The first line defines the input and output function parameters. The function body is embedded between the $$ delimiters and it is written in the procedural language of choice (and we used JavaScript out of the many available PostgreSQL procedural languages). The procedural language identifier is specified after the last $$ delimiter. The IMMUTABLE and STRICT parameters are used by the query planner to optimize the function execution: IMMUTABLE means that for the same input the function will return the same output and STRICT means that for NULL input values the function will return a NULL output. The last line shows how the newly created function is called, using SQL types as parameters.

 We used the previous example from the plv8 documentation available at http://pgxn.org/dist/plv8/doc/plv8.html.

In addition to creating functions using a given procedural function PostgreSQL supports ad hoc execution for code written in a procedural language. We have rewritten the plv8_test() function declaration and invocation as 100% JavaScript code:

```
DO LANGUAGE plv8 $$
    var keys = ['name', 'age'];
    var vals = ['Alex', '37'];
    var o = {};
    for(var i=0; i<keys.length; i++){
        o[keys[i]] = vals[i];
    }
    plv8.elog(NOTICE,JSON.stringify(o));
$$;
```

The elog() function is a plv8 utility function that output a message to the console or the database log. It is similar to the SQL command RAISE. You can find the example in the configureAndTest_plv8.sql file in the postgresql-underscore folder from the source code for this chapter.

Generating data using plv8 and Underscore

We will now take a similar approach with the MongoDB section and create a plv8 version of the code that generates the sample data and stores it in the database. We will also use Underscore in the process and the first two tasks are to create the target table and make Underscore available in the plv8 session:

```
CREATE TABLE IF NOT EXISTS bicycles(
    id int primary key,
    body jsonb not null
);
```

```
CREATE TABLE IF NOT EXISTS js_files(
    id varchar(255) primary key,
    content text not null
);
\set underscore_content `cat node_modules/underscore/underscore.js`

INSERT INTO js_files
SELECT 'underscore', :'underscore_content' WHERE NOT EXISTS(SELECT
id FROM js_files WHERE id = 'underscore');

DO LANGUAGE plv8 $$
  var files = plv8.execute("SELECT content FROM js_files;");
  for (var i = 0; i < files.length; i++)
  {
    var file = files[i].content;
    eval("(function() { " + file + "})")();
  }
$$;
```

We use the second table `js_files` to store the contents of the Underscore file or any other similar library if required. The highlighted line executes an operating system command line and stores the output into a `underscore_content` variable. This is a psql variable and not a SQL variable and it is interpolated into SQL using the `:'underscore_content'` expression as part of the `js_files` table insertion. In this example, the psql variable is declared and initialized within the current script but it can be also be passed as a psql argument.

The plv8 ad hoc code relies on the `plv8.execute()` function to launch a query and read the results as an array of JSON values representing the rows returned by the query. Using the JavaScript `eval()` function, we then parsed and invoked the code read from the file system making Underscore available to the current plv8 session.

We can now proceed to generate some of the example data and insert it into the `bicycles` table using JavaScript. The example was kept as close as possible to the similar example from the MongoDB section and I hope you can recognize most of the code:

```
DO LANGUAGE plv8 $$
  var files = plv8.execute("SELECT content FROM js_files;");
  for (var i = 0; i < files.length; i++)
  {
    var file = files[i].content;
    eval("(function() { " + file + "})")();
  }
```

```
var getBicycles = function() {
  return [{
    id: 1,
    name: "A fast bike",
    type: "Road Bike",
    quantity: 10,
    rentPrice: 20,
    dateAdded: new Date(2015, 1, 2)
  }, {

  ...
  }, {
    id: 12,
    name: "A clown bike",
    type: "Children Bike",
    quantity: 2,
    rentPrice: 12,
    dateAdded: new Date(2014, 11, 1)
  }];
};

if (plv8.execute("SELECT COUNT(*) FROM bicycles;")[0].count ===
0) {
  var bicycles = getBicycles();
  plv8.elog(NOTICE,"Inserting " + bicycles.length + " bicycles
...");
  var sqlScript = "INSERT INTO bicycles VALUES ";
  _.each(bicycles, function (bicycle, index) {
    if(index > 0) {
      sqlScript += ", ";
    }
    sqlScript += "(" + bicycle.id + ", " + "'" +
    JSON.stringify(bicycle) + "')";
  });
  plv8.execute(sqlScript + ";");
} else {
  plv8.elog(NOTICE,"The bicycles collection is not empty.
  Skipping seed data insertion for bicycles.");
}
$$;
```

We used Underscore to build a SQL script based on the bicycles objects converted in the JSON format; after we execute this code out, the `bicycles` table should be populated with the example data. You can find the example in the `insertSeedData.sql` file in the `postgresql-underscore` folder from the source code for this chapter.

The plv8 procedural language looks full of potential for reusing JavaScript code across different functions and database scripts, but it needs a built-in easier way to load JavaScript files.

 You can find the original reference for this example, including a method to preload JavaScript files and make them available to all plv8 sessions, at `http://bit.ly/1bkeUuF`.

Summary

In this chapter, we explored how to use Underscore in different environments starting with the browser with templating support. We then discussed Node.js and described a new way to organize JavaScript code on the server using modules. The last two sections presented two database engines that are JavaScript-friendly and that can launch Underscore as database scripting helper library.

The next chapter will go through some more advanced Underscore topics and will build upon and revisit some concepts that were discussed in this chapter.

6
Related Underscore.js Libraries and ECMAScript Standards

In the previous chapter, we have seen Underscore used across browser, server, and database contexts proving it to be a versatile and essential library. We will now explore some advanced topics for using Underscore such as:

- Alternative and complementary libraries
- The relationship with JavaScript standards and how to write the ECMAScript 2015 (ES6) code

The source code for the examples from this chapter is hosted online at `https://github.com/popalexandruvasile/underscorejs-examples/tree/master/advanced-topics-1` and you can execute the examples using the Cloud9 IDE at `https://ide.c9.io/alexpop/underscorejs-examples/` from the `advanced-topics-1` folder.

Using the Underscore-contrib library

While Underscore is a powerful library and in the same time, it is a relatively small one that has around 1,500 lines of code. You can read through its annotated source code available at `http://underscorejs.org/docs/underscore.html` in less than an hour (if you are an experienced JavaScript developer).

Many popular JavaScript libraries have a similar size and when they become bigger they are split into separate components. These bigger libraries provide some core functionality as a main component and provide further specialized functionality in optional packages.

Underscore-contrib is a functional library that is closely related to Underscore as its official companion or complementary library. The Underscore-contrib source code and documentation are hosted by the same parent organization of Underscore, although a different author created it originally.

Similar to Underscore, it has great documentation and annotated source code available at `http://documentcloud.github.io/underscore-contrib`. Underscore-contrib is dependent on the Underscore library and it provides:

- Specialized functionality that does not belong to Underscore due to its targeted applicability
- Functionality that is more experimental in nature and it should be merged into Underscore after it reaches a certain maturity and acceptance threshold

Underscore-contrib has its functionality split into different components that are contained in one of the 14 JavaScript files that comprise this library. You can reference each file separately and pick and chose the ones that you plan to use. Underscore-contrib also provides a single file that contains all the components for scenarios when you need to use the whole library.

An overview of Underscore-contrib functionality

The library provides distinctive functionality for arrays, collections, functions, objects, and other utility functions that follow closely the areas of functionality already defined in the Underscore documentation (and covered in the first part of this book). In addition to these areas of functionality, Underscore-contrib identifies further units of functionality that map to separate functionality concerns.

We will enumerate the JavaScript files where the Underscore-contrib functionality is contained (this library is using the same _ global object as Underscore to provide its functions). We will only mention a couple of functions for each unit of functionality (followed by some examples in the next subsection):

- `underscore.array.builders.js`: This contains functions that create or construct arrays, such as:
  - `_.cat(...)`: This concatenates zero or more arrays, array-like objects, objects, or a combination of any of these that are passed as parameters into a single array
  - `_.interpose(array, value)`: This returns an array built by inserting the `value` parameter between all the elements of the `array` parameter

- ○ `_.repeat(size, value)`: This returns an array of length equal to the `size` parameter and filled with the `value` parameter

- `underscore.array.selectors.js`: This contains functions that extract values from arrays, such as:

  - ○ `_.best(array, selectFunc)`: This returns the value taken from the `array` parameter that satisfies all calls of the `selectFunc` function parameter over the `array` elements, for example, `selectFunc(elem1, elem2)`, where `elem1` and `elem2` are successive elements from the `array` parameter

  - ○ `_.dropWhile(array, predicate)`: This removes values from the `array` parameter that do not satisfy the `predicate` function until the first element that satisfies it is reached

- `underscore.collections.walk.js`: This contains functions that can traverse and process data from complex JavaScript objects.

- `underscore.function.arity.js`: This contains functions that operate on the arguments of a function by changing the number of arguments (the arity of the function) or by changing how a function and its arguments are evaluated. They create new functions from existing functions. Here are a few examples:

  - ○ `_.binary(func)`: This returns a function that when called with a number of arguments will pass only the first two arguments to the `func` parameter and will discard any other arguments.

  - ○ `_.curry(func[, reverse])`: This returns a new function that is the **curried** version of the `func` parameter function. We already discussed `_.partial()` that binds predefined values to function arguments. The operation of **currying** a function in JavaScript transforms a function and its arguments into a series of nested intermediate functions with one argument (unary functions). We will explore this function in the section examples and I encourage you to explore its theoretical definition at `https://en.wikipedia.org/wiki/Currying`.

- `underscore.function.combinators.js`: This function creates new functions by combining other functions, such as:

  - ○ `_.complement(predicate)`: This creates the reversed equivalent of the `predicate` parameter function

  - ○ `_.conjoin(predicate1[, predicate2[, ..., predicateN]])`: This creates a new predicate function that will filter an array by checking that its elements satisfy all the `predicate1...predicateN` predicates

- `underscore.function.iterators.js`: This contains functions that create collection iterators and functions that operate over these iterators. In this context, an iterator is a function that is based on a collection, and when invoked, it will return the next element from the collection. Here are a couple of examples:
    - `_.iterators.List(array)`: This creates an iterator function from an array. When invoked, the iterator function returns the next element from the `array` parameter and when the last element is reached, it returns `undefined`.
    - `_.iterators.select(iterator, predicate)`: This returns the elements provided by the `iterator` function that satisfy the `predicate` function.

- `underscore.function.predicates.js`: These functions create predicates, such as:
    - `_.isEven(value)`: This returns true if `value` is an even number
    - `_.isJSON(value)`: This returns true if `value` is valid JSON

- `underscore.object.builders.js`: This contains functions that build objects, such as:
    - `_.merge(obj1[, obj2[, ..., objN]])`: This merges two or more objects starting with `object1`
    - `_.snapshot(obj)`: This creates a deep clone of an object

- `underscore.object.selectors.js`: These are functions that extract from objects, such as:
    - `_.kv(obj, key)`: This returns a key-value pair representing a property of `obj` that has a name that matches the `key` parameter
    - `_.pickWhen(obj, predicate)`: This returns a copy of the object `obj` with properties that have values that satisfy the `predicate` function

- `underscore.util.existential.js`: These functions make assertions if an object exists or can be converted to a Boolean value, such as:
    - `_.exists(value)`: This returns `true` if `value` is not equal to `undefined` and not equal to `null`
    - `_.truthy(value)`: This returns true if `value` can be converted to `true`

- `underscore.util.operators.js`: This contains a function that acts as operators, such as:

  - ○ `_.add(value1[, value2[, ..., valueN]])`: This adds all the arguments and returns the result

  - ○ `_.dec(value)`: This decrements the `value` number parameter and returns the result

- `underscore.util.strings.js`: This contains functions that operate on strings, such as:

  - ○ `_.camelCase(value)`: This converts a dash-separated `value` parameter to a camel-cased string. The function `_.toDash(value)` performs the reverse operation.

  - ○ `_.strContains(value, search)`: This returns `true` if the `value` string parameter contains the `search` string parameter.

- `underscore.util.trampolines.js`: This contains functions that enable recursive function behavior while avoiding the JavaScript maximum recursion depth limit for browsers that do not support ECMAScript 2015 (ES6).

We only mentioned a handful of the Underscore-contrib functions to give you an idea of the kind of functionality it offers and how we can adopt a more advanced functional programming style via this library.

> The library author Michael Fogus explores many of its functions and underlying concepts in the book *Functional JavaScript, O'Reilly Media 2013*. This book is strongly recommended if you are interested in adopting a functional programming style with JavaScript.

Exploring Underscore-contrib via examples

To install the library using the Bower package manager, we need to execute the following command line:

```
bower install underscore-contrib --save
```

We will set up a browser-centric project (similar to the ones created for *Chapter 4, Programming Paradigms with Underscore.js*) in the `underscore-contrib` folder from the source code for this chapter. We will use a mix of Underscore and Underscore-contrib functions to illustrate how seamlessly they work together.

We will define a new requirement for a function that concatenates arrays and values into a single sorted array that does not have duplicated values or values that are `null` or `undefined`. The test specification a for this function can be found in the `spec/contribSamplesSpec.js` file:

```
describe("Given contribSamples", function() {
  describe("when calling concatenateArrays()", function() {
    var result = contribSamples.concatenateArrays(1, [5, , 64],
    null, [5,6,7], [1, , 2, null, 3], 99);
    it("then it returns an array of the correct length",
    function() {
      expect(result.length).toEqual(8);
    });
    it("then it returns an array with the correct first and last
    element", function() {
      expect(_.first(result)).toEqual(1);
      expect(_.last(result)).toEqual(99);
    });
  });
});
```

The implementation of this function employs the Underscore-contrib `_.cat()` function to create an initial concatenated array. The initial array is passed to a processing pipeline based on the Underscore `_.chain()` function and the final pipeline value will contain the result array as implemented in the `contribSamples.js` file:

```
var contribSamples = (function() {
  "use strict";

  return {
    concatenateArrays: function(args) {
      var concatResult = _.cat.apply(this, arguments);
      var filteredResult = _.chain(concatResult)
                            .filter(_.existy)
                            .sortBy(_.identity)
                            .unique(true)
                            .value();
      return filteredResult;
    }
  };
}());
```

The two highlighted functions are Underscore-contrib functions, and they don't look out of place with the rest of the Underscore functions. We used the call `_.cat.apply(this, arguments)` to pass the arguments of the outer function unchanged to `_.cat()`. For convenience, you can use the `index.html` file to see the output of this example.

Using the lodash library

The lodash library (`https://lodash.com`) was created as a fork of Underscore, with a focus on better performance, improved consistency across browsers, and enhanced code readability. Currently at version 3, it offers a thorough test suite, excellent documentation, and an extensively customizable build utility. In its previous versions, it even offered an Underscore compatible file so that you can use lodash as a drop-in replacement for Underscore (especially, useful for projects using Backbone.js).

Initially, the main difference between lodash and Underscore was that lodash was not relying on any native JavaScript functions to implement functions such as `_.map()`, `_reduce`, and `_.forEach()`. As discussed in the *Underscore and JavaScript standards* section, Underscore used the native ES5 functions if available (up until version 1.6). These native functions were slower than the lodash equivalent functions, as they catered to many edge cases and historic JavaScript implementations. By using simple loops and modern JavaScript code practices, lodash managed to be significantly faster than Underscore 1.5 and lower. The difference in performance is reduced after Underscore 1.6. As of this version, Underscore follows a similar approach with lodash and drops support for the slow native JavaScript functions. This is one of the reasons that, starting with lodash 3, there is no Underscore-compatible build available anymore.

An overview of lodash functionality

The current version of lodash 3.10 has become (as of July 2015) the most depended upon package on the npm repository overtaking Underscore, which used to hold the top spot before that. The library far exceeds the features of Underscore, as detailed at `https://lodash.com/#features`, and we will explore a couple of them next.

> You can find more information about the differences between Underscore before version 1.6 and lodash in the blog entry at `http://kitcambridge.be/blog/say-hello-to-lo-dash/`. A comparison between Underscore 1.6+ and lodash can be found at `http://benmccormick.org/2014/11/12/underscore-vs-lodash/`.

Functionality-wise, lodash makes the same distinction between areas of concern such as collections, arrays, functions, objects, and utility functions. It refines this distinction by further separating functionality for strings, numbers, dates, and math functions.

For collections, it keeps a common set of functions with Underscore and it defines additional ones, such as:

- `_.at(collection, [props])`: This returns an array of elements that represent either array values or object property values specified as keys or indexed in the optional `props` argument. This argument can be an array of numbers or strings or a comma-delimited list of numbers of strings.

- `_.findLast(collection, [predicate], [thisArg])`: This is similar to `_.find`; it processes the `collection` argument from right to left. We should note that in all lodash functions with optional predicate arguments, the default value is set to the `_.identity` function.

- `_.forEachRight(collection, [iteratee], [thisArg])`: This is similar to lodash `_.forEach()`; it processes the `collection` argument from right to left. Both `_.forEach()` and `_.forEachRight()` functions will stop processing the collection if the `iteratee` function returns `false` and this is another important difference from the Underscore `_.forEach()` implementation.

- `_.sortByOrder(collection, iteratees, [orders])`: This sorts the `collection` argument using `iteratees`, which is an array of functions, property names, or even objects. When `iteratees` contains objects, the properties of each object will be used for comparison against `collection` elements (relying on a function similar to the `_.matches()` utility function for the actual comparison). The optional `orders` argument is an array of Boolean values that specifies the sort order of each `iteratees` entry.

The array functionality has many functions that are similar to Underscore, while also defining new ones, such as:

- `_.chunk(array, [size])`: This splits the `array` argument into arrays of `size` length and returns a new array containing the results.

- `_.dropWhile(array, [predicate], [thisArg])`: This creates a new array without the first elements of the `array` argument that satisfy the `predicate` function. The `predicate` argument can be a string in which case elements are dropped, while they have a property with the same name that evaluates as `true`. If `predicate` is an object, then a function that operates in a similar way with the `_.matches` function will be used to evaluate each element of the `array` argument.

- `_.remove(array, [predicate], [thisArg])`: This mutates the `array` argument and removes the elements that satisfy the `predicate` argument (see `_.dropWhile` for details on how the `predicate` argument is evaluated). The return value is an array containing the removed elements.

- `_.takeWhile(array, [predicate], [thisArg])`: This creates a new array that contains the first elements of the `array` argument that satisfy the `predicate` function (see `_.dropWhile` for details on how the `predicate` argument is evaluated).

Most of the functions that work with objects, strings, numbers, and dates are shared with Underscore, and we can find different ones, such as:

- `_.forOwn(object, [iteratee], [thisArg])`: This is similar to lodash `_.forEach()`; it processes the enumerable properties of the `object` argument (ignoring any inherited enumerable properties).

- `_.mapValues(object, [iteratee=_.identity], [thisArg])`: This is similar to lodash `_.map()`; it creates a version of the `object` argument with the same keys and values generated by the `iteratee` function (its signature is `(value, key, object)`).

- There are string-specific functions that should eliminate the need for a specialized string library, as it is the case for Underscore (see the Underscore string library at https://epeli.github.io/underscore.string/). Here are a couple of useful string-related functions:

    ◦ `_.camelCase([string])`: This converts a string to camel case by changing letters from the Unicode block "Latin-1 Supplement" into letters from the Unicode block "Basic Latin", while removing any combining diacritic marks; for example, `my-custom-control` is converted to `myCustomControl`.

    ◦ `_.padRight([string], [length], [chars])`: This creates a left-padded version from the `string` argument if it is shorter than the `length` argument using the value provided in the `chars` argument.

    ◦ `_.trim([string], [chars])`: This removes the whitespace character at the beginning and at the end of the `string` argument. If the `chars` argument is specified, then the function will remove its characters instead.

    ◦ `_.words([string], [pattern])`: This returns an array of words extracted from the `string` argument. If the `pattern` argument is specified, it will change the default regular expression used by the function to extract the words.

- Number-specific ones such as `_.inRange(n, [start], end)`, which return `true` if n is between `start` and `end-1`.

- Functions for mathematical operations such as `_.sum(collection, [iteratee], [thisArg])`, which calculate the sum of the `collection` element, using the optional `iteratee` function to extract the desired value.

The utility functions have some useful additions on top of the ones shared with Underscore, such as:

- `_.attempt(func)`: This tries to execute the `func` argument function and returns its result or the error raised in the process.

- `_.matches(source)`: This creates a function that performs a deep comparison between its argument and the `source` argument. It is using the enumerable properties of the two objects for comparison, and it even works with arrays.

The area of functionality that targets functions, while similar with Underscore, it differs through API additions like:

- `_.ary(func, [n])`: This creates a version of `func` that only accepts n arguments ignoring the rest.

- `_.curry(func, [arity])`: This creates a curried version of `func` similar to the Underscore-contrib version. The optional `arity` argument controls the depth of nesting, and it defaults to the number of `func` arguments.

- `_.rearg(func, indexes)`: This creates a new function that is a version of `func`, where the new function arguments are mapped back to the `func` arguments via the `indexes` list or array. Each index value is used to locate an argument of the new function that will be passed back to `func` in sequence.

Special mentions should be made for some powerful features from the chaining functionality:

- **Chaining-related functions** allow for a shorter syntax and bring additional functionality compared to Underscore. Rather than using `_.chain(value)` to initiate explicit chaining, you can also use `_(value)` and initiate implicit chaining instead. With implicit chaining, there is no need to call `value()` to terminate the chaining and get the final result from the processing pipeline. The chain will be terminated when a chain method returns a single value or a primitive value.

- **Lazy evaluation** happens when the processing pipeline involved as part of chaining does not create intermediary arrays between successive chain method calls. Instead, there is a process called **shortcut fusion** the where multiple methods of the chain are merged and applied against iterated elements.

- **Deferred execution** is where a chain is not actually executed unless it is terminated explicitly through a `value()` function call, or implicitly by calling a function that returns a single value or a primitive value.

More details about lodash chaining features can be found in the official docs at `https://lodash.com/docs#_` and in the blog entry `http://gajus.com/blog/4/harder-better-faster-stronger-lo-dash-v3#shortcut-fusion`. Further details about lazy evaluation in lodash can be found in the blog entry `http://filimanjaro.com/blog/2014/introducing-lazy-evaluation/`.

There is also a dedicated book for lodash called *Lo-Dash Essentials, Adam Boduch, Packt Publishing,* and you can find more details at `https://www.packtpub.com/web-development/lo-dash-essentials`.

Migrating a project from Underscore to lodash

The lodash library is a great alternative to Underscore offering many more features, better performance, and finer grained control on what gets imported from this library. Many Underscore users have switched to lodash because of its benefits, so we will discuss the migration process.

To illustrate how easy is to switch from Underscore to lodash for an existing project, we will reuse the one found in the `oop-underscore` folder from the source code for *Chapter 4, Programming Paradigms with Underscore.js*. The converted project can be found in the folder `lodash-migration` from the source code for this chapter.

To install the library using the Bower package manager, we need to execute the following command line:

```
bower install lodash --save
```

The next step is to replace all references to the Underscore library file with references to the lodash library file in `index.html` and in `SpecRunner.html` files. If we run the tests by opening the `SpecRunner.html` file in the browser, we will notice that they are all successful. This is a scenario where having tests in place helps us migrate code across different libraries or different versions of the same library.

However, if we open the `index.html` file, there is no rendered content displayed. This is caused by an exception in the `index.js` file, as the `_.first(array)` function in lodash only returns the first element of an array. To fix the error, we need to replace the Underscore call `_.first(contacts, 4)` with its lodash equivalent `_.take(contacts, 4)`.

 The lodash library has a dedicated page for the migration from Underscore at `https://github.com/lodash/lodash/wiki/Migrating`.

Underscore and JavaScript standards

Up until Underscore 1.6, there was a strong correlation between the library and some of the native JavaScript functions available in ES5. Starting with Underscore 1.7, this link was broken and the library introduced implementations that performed better than the native JavaScript equivalents. For example, the native JavaScript functions operating on arrays make provisions for so called **sparse arrays**. In JavaScript, arrays behave similarly to objects: they can contain elements at arbitrary indexes even if the initial length is less than the index value, as shown in this code snippet:

```
var arr = [];
arr[5] = null;
arr[12] = 1;
console.log("Array length is " + arr.length);
```

The array length is now 13, and as it only contains two defined elements, we say that the array is sparse. Prior to Underscore 1.7, enumerating a sparse array using the `_.each()` function would only touch the valid elements from the array, and this involves extra computational effort. Starting with version 1.7, Underscore treats all arrays as dense arrays or arrays that are expected to contain values at all their indexes. Using Underscore 1.8 or greater means that enumerating the sparse array from the previous example would touch elements at all 13 indexes, even if most of them were not defined. This change makes Underscore slightly faster than the equivalent ECMAScript functions, and at the same time incompatible with them.

For brevity, we will refer to ECMAScript 5.1 as ES5 throughout the rest of the chapter.

ECMAScript 5.1 (ES5)

The following functions were first standardized in ES5 and are similar with Underscore functions:

- `Array.prototype.forEach()` is similar to `_.each()`
- `Array.prototype.map()` is similar to `_.map()`
- `Array.prototype.reduce()` is similar to `_.reduce()`
- `Array.prototype.reduceRight()` is similar to `_.reduceRight()`
- `Array.prototype.filter()` is similar to `_.filter()`
- `Array.prototype.every()` is similar to `_.every()`
- `Array.prototype.some()` is similar to `_.some()`
- `Array.prototype.indexOf()` is similar to `_.indexOf()`
- `Array.prototype.lastIndexOf()` is similar to `_.lastIndexOf()`

Underscore functions are faster than their native JavaScript equivalent; they work with objects and array-like instances, and they support chaining.

There are also ES5 functions that will be used by Underscore instead of its own implementation if defined in the JavaScript engine executing the code:

- `Array.isArray()` is equivalent to `_.isArray()`
- `Object.keys()` is equivalent to `_.keys()`
- `Function.prototype.bind()` is equivalent to `_.bind()`
- `Object.create()` is used in the Underscore function `_.create()`

Overall, Underscore is closely aligned with ES5, and while it cannot be used as a direct replacement anymore, it is a library that can be used to write modern JavaScript code in the spirit of ES5.

ECMAScript 2015 (ES6)

The sixth edition of the ECMA-262 standard is also known as ES6, and it was finalized and released officially in June 2015 as the "**ECMAScript 2015 Language Specification**". The emphasis on a year of release rather than a version number is in line with the plans to have yearly iterations for the standard that defines the JavaScript language. The next version of JavaScript should be standardized as **ECMAScript 2016 (ES7)** and be finalized at some point in 2016. For brevity, we will use the ES6 acronym each time we refer to the ECMAScript 2015 standard, as it is a widely used moniker.

ES6 contains a series of features that make JavaScript an expressive and powerful language, in line with other programming languages such as Java, C#, or Ruby. Some of the most important features introduced in ES6 are modules and classes, and these features resolve the biggest shortcomings of JavaScript as a language by introducing native support for encapsulation and modularity. Given the renewed effort to standardize new features in ECMAScript on a yearly basis, I think that ES6 adoption should be a top priority for any new JavaScript project. A modern JavaScript library such as Underscore benefits considerably from ES6 features, and we will focus a large part of the rest of the book on the topic of ES6 adoption.

We will start by mentioning some of the new additions in ES6, followed by an exploration of some of these additions.

Array – new features

First, we will highlight the ES6 new features for the `Array` object as they complement or replace some of the Underscore functionality.

There are new static methods for the `Array` object that make it easier to create array instances:

- `Array.from(items[, mapfn[, thisArg]])`: `items` is an array-like object that will be converted to an `Array` instance. The second optional argument `mapfn` is a mapping function that operates on each element of the array. The third optional argument `thisArg` represents the `this` value for the `mapfn` function. `Array.from()` is similar to `_.toArray()`. Here is an example showcasing its functionality:

```
var arrayFromDemo = function(n1, n2, n3, n4) {
  console.log("arguments length: " + arguments.length);
  console.log("Is arguments an instance of Array? " +
  (arguments instanceof Array));
  var argsArray = Array.from(arguments);
  console.log("argsArray length: " + argsArray.length);
  console.log("Is argsArray an instance of Array? " +
  (argsArray instanceof Array));
};
arrayFromDemo(1, 2, 3, 4);
// "arguments length: 4"
// "Is arguments an instance of Array? false"
// "argsArray length: 4"
// "Is argsArray an instance of Array? true"
```

- `Array.of(argument0, [argument1, [..., [argumentN]]])`: This function converts consecutive arguments into an array, as exemplified in the following code snippet. This function eliminates the need to use the `_.toArray()` function for scenarios when we need to create an `Array` instance from function parameters:

```
var arrayOfDemo = function(n1, n2, n3, n4) {
  var argsArray = Array.of(n1, n2, n3 , n4);
  console.log("argsArray length: " + argsArray.length);
  console.log("Is argsArray an instance of Array? " + (argsArray
instanceof Array));
};
arrayOfDemo(1,2,3,4);
// "argsArray length: 4"
// "Is argsArray an instance of Array? true"
```

There are also new instance methods for the `Array` object that can replace or complement some of the Underscore functionality:

- `Array.prototype.copyWithin(target, start [,end])`: This copies values from the array at the `start` index to array positions starting with the `target` index. This function does not have a similar Underscore alternative.

- `Array.prototype.entries()`: This returns an `Array` iterator object that can be enumerated by calling its `next()` method or through the new ES6 `for...of` statement. The iterated item contains an array object that holds the item index and the item value as elements. The functionality is somewhat similar to the `_.pairs(object)` function with the main difference that the former function works with arrays and the latter with objects.

- `Array.prototype.fill(value[, start[, end]])`: This function copies the `value` argument from the `start` index to the `end` index of the array. If `end` is not specified, it will be set to the last index of the array. Again, this function does not have an Underscore alternative.

- `Array.prototype.find(predicate[, thisArg])`: This is similar to `_.find()`.

- `Array.prototype.findIndex(predicate[, thisArg])`: This is similar to `_.findIndex()`.

- `Array.prototype.keys()`: This returns an `Array` iterator object and the iterated item contains the index value of the current array element. The functionality is somewhat similar to the `_.keys(object)` function and the main difference is that the ES6 function works with arrays and the Underscore one with objects.

- `Array.prototype.values()`: This returns an `Array` iterator object and the iterated item contains the value of the current array element. The functionality is somewhat similar to the `_.values(object)` function and the main difference is that the ES6 function works with arrays and the Underscore one with objects.

Other notable new features

Next, we will highlight a couple of new language features that have significant implications on JavaScript development, and we will explore them later through a series of examples:

- Support for classes and modules:
  - ° We can declare classes and use prototype-based inheritance explicitly via constructors and base class calls
  - ° Modules help us organize code and solve the problem of exporting data and functionality in an elegant manner

- Arrow functions (or fat arrow functions or lambda functions): These functions can be expressed using a more concise syntax (similar to the syntax for anonymous functions in C# or Java). The arrow functions have the `this` variable set to the `this` variable of its surrounding context, rather than defining their own value as in the classic function behavior.

- Support for block-scoped variables through `let` and `const` keywords. We don't have to worry about the pollution of global scope or accidentally overriding values that should be read only.

- Template strings and object literal enhancements (support for the `__proto__` keyword and a more concise way to declare variables and functions).

- Function arguments: default values, better handling through rest and spread features.

- Among many other features, we should mention the introduction of promises, extensive destructuring support, iterators and generators, new data structures such as `Map`, `Set`, `WeakMap`, and `WeakSet`, reflection support, and proxies.

Before seeing some of these features in action, we will discuss various options to execute ES6 code, and we will set up a development workflow that will be iterated upon in the next and final chapter.

You can find more about the **ECMAScript 2015 (ES6)** standard from its official documentation at `http://www.ecma-international.org/ecma-262/6.0/index.html`. There is a lot of online material about ES6 that reflects the community interest, and I will mention just a few resources: an overview of its most important features at `https://github.com/lukehoban/es6features#readme`; a series of blog posts at `https://hacks.mozilla.org/category/es6-in-depth/`; the books *Exploring ES6* by Axel Rauschmayer available at `http://exploringjs.com/es6/`; and *Understanding ES6* by Nicholas C. Zakas available at `https://leanpub.com/understandinges6/read/`.

Using ECMAScript 2015 (ES6) today with transpilers

At the moment of writing the book, none of the major browsers had full support for ES6. However, there is lot of progress in this space and it might be possible that at the time you are reading this book at least one major browser (if not all) will fully support ES6. A good way to track progress of the ES6 support in browsers and JavaScript runtimes is through the compatibility table at `https://kangax.github.io/compat-table/es6/`. For example, Google Chrome, Mozilla Firefox and Microsoft Edge (the new browser that replaces Internet Explorer in Windows 10) had at least 60% support for ES6 in July 2015, while Safari 8 and Internet Explorer 11 had less than 20% support.

Until support for ES6 is widely available, a good solution to adopt ES6 is to use a transpiler (a shorter word for transcompiler), which is a special type of compiler that transforms code between two languages that are similar. These transpilers convert code from ES6, or other upcoming ECMAScript specifications such as ECMASCript 2016 (ES7) into code that is compatible with older specifications such as ES5 or ES3. They usually support many configurations options that will allow you to specify the target specification and whether you convert each file in its own output file or in one single output file among other things.

Two popular transpilers that convert ES6 or ES7 are Google Traceur (more information available at `https://github.com/google/traceur-compiler/wiki/Getting-Started`) and Babel (formerly known as 6to5) available at `http://babeljs.io`.

Babel experienced a great increase in community adoption in 2015, and as of July 2015, it has the most comprehensive support for ES6 at 73%. We will use this transpiler throughout the book to convert any ES6 code to its ES5 equivalent.

Using Babel directly in the browser

Babel can be used in a browser environment without an explicit transpilation step. First, we need to install the `babel-core` npm module in the project folder using the following command line:

```
npm install babel-core --save
```

The module contains two files that are required next:

- The `browser.js` file, which will transform the ES6 code into ES5 code on the fly.

- The `browser-polyfill.js` file, which provides support for nontrivial ES6 features such as generator, iterators, promises, and others. It is based on two projects: regenerator (`https://github.com/facebook/regenerator`), which provides support for ES6 generator functions, and core-js (`https://github.com/zloirock/core-js`), which provides support for ES6 symbols, collections, iterators, and promises among other features.

These two files need to be included in the `<head>` element at the top of the HTML file that contains the ES6 code. The ES6 code needs to be provided inline in the same file inside a `<script type="text/ecmascript-6">` or a `<script type="text/babel">` element.

Our ES6 example shows two classes, one derived from the other and a `Set` object that requires the `browser-polyfill.js` file to work as expected. A class in ES6 can use a `constructor` function for initialization and can be derived from another class using the `extends` keyword. The functionality around classes in ES6 should be familiar as it is very close to what we covered in *Chapter 4, Programming Paradigms with Underscore.js*. The `Set` object holds a collection of unique values and any duplicate value added to it will be ignored.

Here are the contents of `index.html` file for the folder `babel-client` found in the source code for this chapter:

```html
<!DOCTYPE html>
<html>
<head>
  <title>Using Babel in the browser without transpilation</title>
  <script src="bower_components/jquery/dist/jquery.js"></script>
  <script src="node_modules/babel-core/browser.js"></script>
  <script src="node_modules/babel-core/browser-polyfill.js"></script>
</head>
<body>
  <h1>Example output:</h1>
```

```
<div id="output"></div>
<script type="text/ecmascript-6">
  class Greeter {
    constructor(message) {
      this.message = message;
    }
    getMessage() {
      return "An instance of class " + this.constructor.name + "
      says: " + this.message;
    }
  }
  class DerivedGreeter extends Greeter {
    constructor(message) {
      super(message + " !");
    }
  }
  let aGreeter = new DerivedGreeter("Hello world");
  let message = aGreeter.getMessage();
  var aSet = new Set([10, 20, 30, 40, 50, 10, 20, 30]);
  $("#output").html(message + "<br /> The example set size is "
  + aSet.size);
</script>
</body>
</html>
```

I have highlighted the HTML elements required by Babel, and if you open the file in a browser, you should see the correct output:

An instance of class DerivedGreeter says: Hello world !

The example set size is 5

This approach is not recommended for writing production code, and you should only use it as a quick way to write ES6 code. I would use this example as a starter project for learning and testing ES6 or ECMAScript 2017 (ES7) functionality without employing a complicated workflow.

Babel is currently provided through npm packages, and in this example, we had to use both Bower and npm to manage our dependencies. We will show a better way to automate the build process in *Chapter 7, Underscore.js Build Automation and Code Reusability*.

An overview of Babel CLI

Babel can be used to transpile ES6 in a browser environment or in a Node.js environment using a **CLI** (**command-line interface**) package via the npm module called `babel`. It is recommended that you install Babel as a global npm module using the following command line:

```
npm install babel --global
```

You can now use the `babel` executable and start transpiling ES6 code to ES5 using a workflow configured, as following:

- A one-to-one file mapping where each ES6 file has an ES5 equivalent file. This is a suitable setup for Node.js code. You could also use this setup in a browser environment for specific development deployments, but you need to ensure when deploying to production that you don't link to too many files. You could also have an automated build step where you can concatenate the generated ES5 files and we will explore these options in *Chapter 7, Underscore.js Build Automation and Code Reusability*.

- A many-to-one file mapping, where all of the ES6 files get converted to one ES5 file, and this is a suitable approach when deploying to a browser environment.

- In a server-side environment you can write code using ES6 language features and execute your Node.js program using the Babel enabled executable:

```
babel-node index.js
```

- Executing `babel-node` will start a Babel enabled Node.js interactive session, where you can write ES6 code directly.

- Using a require hook that will bind to the Node.js module system and transpile ES6 files dynamically.

We will explore some of these options in the next sections with a view to establishing a workflow that can be used to explore some of the ES6 features.

Using Babel CLI for the client-side code

We will modify the previous example from the `babel-client` folder and move the JavaScript code from the `index.html` file into separate files in the `es6` folder found in `babel-client-cli` from the source code for this chapter. The classes are now in their own file `es6/greeters.es6` and the code that generates the example output is in `es6/index.es6`. Notice that we used the `.es6` extension that is supported by Babel for the code written in ES6, but we could have used the `.js` extension or even a custom one that can be declared in the Babel configuration.

At this point, we have our ES6 files ready and we can transpile them into the ES5 equivalent by running the next command with the target folder es6 as the first argument:

```
babel es6 --watch --out-dir es5
```

The second argument `--watch` will ensure that any change in the es6 folder will trigger a new transpilation and the last argument `--out-dir es5` sets the destination folder. After running this command, you should see the following folder structure in the `babel-client-cli` folder:

```
├── es5
│   ├── greeters.js
│   └── index.js
├── es6
│   ├── greeters.es6
│   └── index.es6
├── index-with-many-files.html
└── index-with-one-file.html
```

If you open the `index-with-many-files.html` file in a browser, you should see the same output as in the previous example from the `babel-client` folder. Also, the `index-with-many-files.html` file links to all the files from the es5 folder.

Babel can transpile all the files from a folder in a single file, and this is the required command:

```
babel es6 --watch --out-file es5/app.js
```

The `index-with-one-file.html` file links to a generated file and displays the expected output when opened in a browser. This example is provided as a way of comparing ES6 code with its converted ES5 output, and it should not be used for production code as it lacks the integration with a module system.

ES6 brings the powerful structural construct of `module` that is similar to the Node.js module, but the specification that defines the module loader has not made it into the final version. It was separated instead into its own specification at `http://whatwg.github.io/loader/`, and we will explore using a module loader in *Chapter 7, Underscore.js Build Automation and Code Reusability.*

Using Babel with Node.js

When working in a Node.js environment, Babel provides a require hook that integrates in the runtime module system and provides dynamic transpilation. We will evolve our previous example and move each class into its own file and use the new ES6 module syntax in the process. Before we progress with the example, we need to install Babel as an npm module that is local to the current example folder to support the `require()` hook:

```
npm install babel --save
```

We already discussed the CommonJS module system used by Node.js in *Chapter 5, Using Underscore.js in the Browser, on the Server, and with the Database* and this module system is synchronous and has a compact syntax. At this point, we should mention another module system used in browser environments called AMD (asynchronous module definition) and implemented by the library RequireJS available at `http://requirejs.org/`. The AMD module system loads modules asynchronously and supports dynamic module configuration while being more verbose than CommonJS.

The ES6 module system is reconciling both these systems and has support for synchronous and asynchronous loading, has a compact syntax, can handle cyclic dependencies, and enables dynamic module configuration.

The ES6 module system should feel very similar to CommonJS as each ES6 module maps to one JavaScript file, and it supports many named exports and one default export per file. We have converted the `Greeter` class to an ES6 module that exports the class definition as default:

```
export default class Greeter {
  constructor(message) {
    this.message = message;
  }
  getMessage() {
    return "An instance of class " + this.constructor.name + "
    says: " + this.message;
  }
}
```

The `DerivedGreeter` class is a module that imports the `Greeter` class, and it also exports its own class definition as default:

```
import Greeter from './Greeter';
export default class DerivedGreeter extends Greeter {
```

```
    constructor(message) {
      super(message + " !");
    }
  }
}
```

Notice the keywords `import` and `export` that make the module declaration explicit and easy to read. You can find the section example in the `babel-server` folder from the source code for this chapter. The ES6 modules can be found in the `es6` folder and they use the `.es6` extension to differentiate from regular JavaScript code.

When Babel processes ES6 module files, it will transpile them by default as CommonJS modules. Because of this behavior, we can reference Node.js modules such as Underscore using the ES6 module syntax. We will import Underscore as an npm package in our example folder using the command:

npm install underscore --save

Next, in the `es6/example.es6` file, we will import Underscore as an ES6 module and define the current module that contains both a default and a named export:

```
import DerivedGreeter from './DerivedGreeter';
import _ from "underscore";

export let name = "example";
export default function getExampleOutput() {
  let aGreeter = new DerivedGreeter("Hello world");
  let message = aGreeter.getMessage();

  let aSet = new Set([10, 20, 30, 40, 50, 10, 20, 30]);
  var arrayFromSet = Array.from(aSet);
  var size = _.size(arrayFromSet);
  return message + ". The example set size is: " + aSet.size + ".
  The example set size calculated with underscore is: " + size;
}
```

We used both the `Set.size` property and the `_.size()` function to calculate the dimension of the `aSet` instance to showcase the use of ES6 features alongside a popular JavaScript library, such as Underscore.

To execute this example, we have two options:

- Use an ES6 code file called by the `babel-node` executable. This file will use the ES6 module syntax to load and execute the `example` module.

- Use the Babel require hook in a regular Node.js code file called by the node executable. This file will use the Node.js require syntax to load and execute the `example` module.

For the first option, we will use the `index.es6` file to import both the default and named exports from the `example` module:

```
import { default as getExampleOutput, name } from './es6/example';
console.log(name + " - " + getExampleOutput());
```

The import expression from `index.es6` cannot use `default` as a reference and has to rename it as `getExampleOutput`. To execute the file, we need to run this command in the sample folder:

```
babel-node index.es6
```

The sample output is slightly different to include the Underscore call result and the named export property value:

```
example - An instance of class DerivedGreeter says: Hello world !. The
example set size is: 5. The example set size calculated with underscore
is: 5
```

For the second option, we will use the `index.js` file to configure the Babel require hook and load the `example` module:

```
require("babel/register")({
    only: /es6/
});

var example = require("./es6/example");
var getExampleOutput = example.default;

console.log(example.name + " - " + getExampleOutput());
```

The first `require` method is the Babel require hook that supports many configuration options, and we used the `only` configuration that enforces the dynamic transpilation for files that match a specific regex. Some default configuration options exclude the `node_modules` folder from transpilation and restrict the file extensions that are processed by Babel, but they can be changed easily and you can find more details at `http://babeljs.io/docs/usage/require/`. The second `require()` loads the ES6 module that, in fact, is transpiled by Babel as a CommonJS module so that it can be consumed natively in Node.js. You can find more details about modules transpilation with Babel at `https://babeljs.io/docs/usage/modules/`.

To execute the example, we need to run the following command line:

```
node index.js
```

We have now established a couple of Babel enabled workflows and each one can be used as a quick and relatively simple starting point to explore ES6 features.

ECMAScript 2015 (ES6) by example

Using ES6 today via a tool such as Babel is a great way to write modern JavaScript code and prepare for the moment when browsers and runtimes will fully support the new specification. Microsoft Edge, Google Chrome, and Mozilla Firefox are on track to become fully ES6 compatible by early 2016 if not faster. The Node.js project has released a new major version (Node 4.0 in September 2015) that incorporates Google Chrome V8 engine changes a lot faster than its previous versions and this also includes new ES6 features. This is the reason why ES6 should be used now rather than later and this is also why we explored the capabilities of a tool such as Babel that makes ES6 possible on any JavaScript engine.

We will continue exploring other ES6 features and we will use the Node.js Babel integration facilitated by the `babel-node` executable. This is the simplest way to execute ES6 code, and it does not involve additional steps or switching context between ES6 and ES5. We rely on the CommonJS module system that is also the current default module system supported by Babel.

In the process of setting up Babel, we already explored some of the ES6 features: classes, modules, and the `Set` structure. We also used the `Array.from()` expression to convert a `Set` object to an `Array` object. `Set` is an iterable object and `Array.from()` will convert these types of object to `Array`. Iterators and generator are not covered in this book, but you can find more information in the ES6 reference materials already mentioned or at `https://developer.mozilla.org/en-US/docs/Web/JavaScript/Guide/Iterators_and_Generators`.

Another ES6 feature that we used in our examples was the `let` keyword that helps enforcing block scopes for variables. In ES5, you had two scopes: the global scope and function scope, and in ES6, there is an additional block scope. Variables defined with `let` have block scope — that is, when defined inside an `if` or a `for` statement, they are only visible and accessible inside that statement scope (which is what we refer to as a block scope).

A great reference for exploring ES6 features is the Mozilla Developer Network documentation available at `https://developer.mozilla.org`. I recommend that you use it as the starting point for any JavaScript-related query and ES6 in particular. You can also use the two books I mentioned at the beginning of the section for a more in-depth explanation.

Testing ES6 code

As an additional step, we will add unit testing support similar to the Node.js unit testing from *Chapter 5, Using Underscore.js in the Browser, on the Server, and with the Database*. There is an npm package called `jasmine-es6` that integrates with Babel and provides a Jasmine executable that can run tests written in the ES6 syntax (the project is hosted at `https://github.com/vinsonchuong/jasmine-es6`). We will adapt and slightly change the example from the `babel-server` folder into a starter for the rest of the ES6 examples. First of all, we need to install the `jasmine-es6` npm package using the following command:

```
npm install jasmine-es6 --save-dev
```

At this point, we have a Jasmine executable that is ES6 aware and we can initialize the test configuration files by running the next command:

```
node_modules/.bin/jasmine init
```

The generated file `spec/support/jasmine.json` needs to have this content:

```
{
  "spec_dir": "spec",
  "spec_files": [
    "**/*[sS]pec.js",
    "**/*[sS]pec.es6"
  ],
  "helpers": [
    "../node_modules/jasmine-es6/lib/install.js",
    "helpers/**/*.js"
  ]
}
```

Notice that the `spec_files` node accepts the `.es6` extension and we added an additional line to the `helpers` node that is required by `jasmine-es6` to work properly.

All the ES6 examples from this section reside in the `es6/examples.es6` file and they have a matching `spec/examplesSpec.es6` file that contains the test specifications. You can find the examples in the `es6-examples` folder from the source code for this chapter and its folder structure should look like the following (excluding the `node_modules` folder, which is not shown):

```
├── es6
│   ├── DerivedGreeter.es6
│   ├── Greeter.es6
```

```
|        └── examples.es6
├── spec
|    ├── support
|    |    └── jasmine.json
|    └── examplesSpec.es6
└── package.json
```

We have slightly changed the es6/examples.es6 file to use named function exports for each ES6 feature: getDerivedGreeterMessage() for the classes and getSetSize() for the Set object.

Before looking at the test specifications, you can also execute some of the examples invoked in the index.es6 file by running the following command in the example folder:

babel-node index.es6

The spec/examplesSpec.es6 file is targeting the named exports from the es6/examples.es6 file to define the following test specifications:

```
import * as examples from '../es6/examples';

describe('Given examples module', function() {
  it('when calling getDerivedGreeterMessage() then returns the
  correct result', () => {
    const message = examples.getDerivedGreeterMessage();
    expect(message).toBe('An instance of class DerivedGreeter says:
    Hello world !');
  });

  it('when calling getSetSize() then returns the correct result', ()
  => {
    const setSizeInfo = examples.getSetSize();
    expect(setSizeInfo).toBe('The example set size is: 5. The example
    set size calculated with underscore is: 5');
  });
});
```

Notice the use of the ES6 const keyword that is similar to let in having block scope visibility, but it cannot be reassigned or redeclared after initialization.

To execute the tests, we need to invoke the jasmine-es6 executable with the following command and watch the two test cases passing:

node_modules/.bin/jasmine

Further ES6 examples – the arrow function

We have already used classes and one of the new static `Array` object methods `Array.from()` in our current example. We will showcase next an important new feature in E6 known as the **arrow function**. An arrow function is an anonymous function declared using a shorter syntax and for which the `this` reference is bound to its surrounding context. As discussed previously for regular functions in ES6, the `this` reference can hold different values depending of context and with arrow function this issue is resolved.

To show this functionality, we will define an `ArrayAccumulator` class that takes an array of numbers and a maximum value as its constructor arguments and adds a value to each element of the array until the maximum value is reached:

```
export default class ArrayAccumulator {
  constructor(seedArray, maxValue) {
    this.values = seedArray;
    this.maxValue = maxValue;
  }
  addToArray(addedValue) {
    this.values.forEach((value, index) => {
      if (value === this.maxValue) {
        return;
      }
      value += addedValue;
      if (value > this.maxValue) {
        value = maxValue;
      }
      this.values[index] = value;
    });
  }
}
```

The first highlighted code snippet shows the declaration of the arrow function, and the second highlighted one has the `this` reference. If we had used a regular anonymous function instead, then the `this.maxValue` variable would be `undefined` and the example would fail when executing the test specification defined in the `spec/ArrayAccumulatorSpec.es6` file.

The arrow function should prove invaluable when working with Underscore functions in an ES6 context and when using it inside classes.

Further ES6 examples – function declaration improvements

There are a series of changes that facilitate calling functions and manipulating functions arguments. Function arguments support default values in ES6 and we can write the constructor for the `ArrayAccumulator` class to support this feature:

```
export default class ArrayAccumulator {
  constructor(seedArray, maxValue = 100) {
    ...
  }
  ...
}
```

If we initialize a class instance using expressions such as new `ArrayAccumulator([1,2,3])` or new `ArrayAccumulator([1,2,3],undefined)`, then the `maxValue` parameter will take the default value of 100.

Function declarations also support the ES6 **rest operator** that represents an array of a variable number of arguments. Here is the rest operator in the highlighted code from the following function (added to the `es6/examples.es6` file):

```
export function functionUsingRestOperator(argsNo, ...otherArgs) {
  if (otherArgs.length + 1 !== argsNo) {
    return "Incorrect number of required arguments. Expected " +
    argsNo + " and " + arguments.length + " were supplied.";
  }
  if (arguments.length < 2) {
    return "Too few arguments were supplied.";
  }
  return arguments.length;
}
```

The example is using the `otherArgs` parameter to ensure the number of arguments matches expectations. Next, we have a test specification that calls the function using regular parameters followed by a test specification that uses the **spread operator**. The spread operator transforms an iterable object into a comma separated list of items, such as the one expected by a function call or an array literal declaration. The highlighted code in the following snippet shows the spread operator in action:

```
describe('when calling functionUsingRestOperator()', () => {
  ...
  describe('with correct number of arguments', () => {
    let result = examples.functionUsingRestOperator(4, {
```

```
          id: 1
      }, {
          id: 2
      }, {
          id: 3
      });
      it('then returns the argument length', () => {
        expect(result).toBe(4);
      });
    });
    describe('with the spread operator', () => {
      let argsArray = [4, {
          id: 1
      }, {
          id: 2
      }, {
          id: 3
      }];

      let result = examples.functionUsingRestOperator(...argsArray);
      it('should return the argument length', () => {
        expect(result).toBe(4);
      });
    });
  });
```

I hope this section provided an initial encounter with some of the ES6 features and made a strong case for ES6 adoption. There are many more ES6 features that will help when working with Underscore on the client or on the server, and I recommend exploring them using the additional reference material that was mentioned in this section.

Summary

We started the chapter by exploring the complementary library underscore-contrib and the alternative library lodash. We then discussed the Underscore functions that are similar with the ones standardized in the ES5 and ES6 specifications, and we focused on presenting some of the ES6 features that facilitate and simplify working with Underscore.

Writing code using ES6 syntax is key for becoming more productive in JavaScript, and we explored a couple of workflows based on Babel that enable most of the ES6 features today in the client and on the server. The next chapter will discuss how to automate JavaScript code-related tasks and how to reuse code between a client and server environments using both ES5 and ES6 focused approaches.

7
Underscore.js Build Automation and Code Reusability

In the previous chapter, we discussed Underscore.js-related libraries, ECMAScript standards, and how to use ES6. We will now explore other advanced topics for using Underscore, such as:

- Build automation with Gulp.js
- Reusing code between client and server environments

The source code for the examples from this chapter is hosted online at `https://github.com/popalexandruvasile/underscorejs-examples/tree/master/advanced-topics-2`, and you can execute the examples using the Cloud9 IDE at the address `https://ide.c9.io/alexpop/underscorejs-examples/` from the `advanced-topics-2` folder.

Build automation with Gulp

So far, all the examples that targeted the browser environment took more effort to configure and execute compared with the examples targeting Node.js. The lack of a dynamic module system is one of the reasons for all the additional steps, and it may take a while until all the major browsers will natively support ES6 modules.

Another important consideration is the need to reduce the number of resource requests when deploying to the browser environment and usually this is accomplished through file concatenation using a build automation tool (also known as a build system or a task runner). Many server-side web application frameworks already have their own build systems, such as Rake for the programming language Ruby, while JavaScript has its own build systems powered by Node.js. Two of the more popular ones are Grunt (http://gruntjs.com/) and Gulp.js (http://gulpjs.com). We will use Gulp in this chapter to automate some manual tasks from one of our previous examples.

Gulp is a code-driven build system based on Node.js streams that provides a simple API comprised of just four functions. Additional functionality is available through a rich plugin ecosystem, and you will see some of the plugins used in the example for this section.

To start using Gulp, we will use the browser-underscore example from *Chapter 5, Using Underscore.js in the Browser, on the Server, and with the Database*, and transform it into the gulp-automation example that can be found into the source code for this chapter. First, we will move all the example JavaScript code in the app folder leaving the test specifications where they are. Next, we will install Gulp as a global npm module so that it becomes available as a command-line tool:

```
npm install gulp --global
```

Then, we will install Gulp as a current project module, so we can load it as a Node.js module:

```
npm install gulp --save-dev
```

Gulp expects a file called gulpfile.js to be present in the current project folder, and we will start with the simplest one possible:

```
var gulp = require('gulp');
gulp.task('default', function() {
  // place code for your default task here
});
```

Notice how the module gulp was used to invoke the core API function gulp.task(name[, deps], fn). The first argument defines the name of the current task, the optional deps argument is an array of task names that will be executed before the current task, and the last argument is the function that defines the current task. If we execute gulp in the command line, you will see log messages stating that the task default is invoked successfully and nothing else.

We will now define the first real task that will concatenate all the files in the `app` folder into a single `public/app.js` file. We will use two more Gulp functions:

- `gulp.src(globs[, options])` returns a stream representing a selection of files so that it can be processed further. The first argument `globs` can be single value or an array of values. These values, also known as `globs`, represent a path to a file or a folder or a pattern matching files using the command shell syntax found in Mac OS X and Linux systems (you can find more details at `https://github.com/isaacs/node-glob`, which is an npm module used by Gulp for this function).
- `gulp.dest(path[, options])` outputs the files contained in the processed stream to a folder or a virtual file depending on the type of the path argument. If `path` is a string, it writes to the location defined by it and returns the current stream, so it can be processed further (for other usage scenarios including output to a virtual file that we will not cover here, please see `https://github.com/gulpjs/gulp/blob/master/docs/API.md`).

To use the concatenation module, we will install a Gulp plugin provided as an npm module using the following command:

```
npm install gulp-concat --save-dev
```

Here is the first task of the `gulpfile.js` that creates the `public/app.js` file:

```
var gulp = require('gulp');
var concat = require('gulp-concat');
gulp.task('build-app', function() {
  gulp.src('app/**/*.js')
    .pipe(concat('app.js'))
    .pipe(gulp.dest('./public/'));
});
```

The `pipe()` function is a Node.js stream API function that is used to transfer data between streams: `pipe()` is invoked on the current stream with the argument function `concat()` that returns a writable stream. The `pipe()` call will transfer copy the current stream to the writable stream. We will not cover Node.js streams here, but you can use `https://nodejs.org/api/stream.html` as a reference. If we execute the following command line, we will see the new file created as `public/app.js`:

```
gulp build-app
```

The first automation step allows us to replace all individual JavaScript file references from the `index.html` file with a single reference to a bundle file that contains all the application code. Any file added in the `app` folder will be automatically included in the bundle and a further step could minimize the bundle, so it can be deployed in a production environment.

Ideally, we should be able to use the same bundle file when executing the test specifications for this example, but the `app/index.js` file included there will cause errors. Our tests are unit tests where we try and test specific functionality from a JavaScript file and the `index.js` file relies on the HTML document object model to be present and libraries such as jQuery to be made available. Testing the `index.js` file brings us into end-to-end or integration tests territory that we will not cover here. To focus only on unit tests, we need to create a bundle that excludes the `index.js` file, and we will use another Gulp plugin called gulp-ignore, which is available as an npm module. The following command will install it for our example:

```
npm install gulp-ignore --save-dev
```

We can now exclude a given glob from a `gulp.src()` files selection by prefixing it with the `!` character. Here is the task that creates the bundle that can be used for testing the application code:

```
gulp.task('build-tests', function() {
  gulp.src([appScripts, '!app/index.js'])
    .pipe(concat('app.js'))
    .pipe(gulp.dest('./spec/public/'));
});
```

By running this task, we will create a file that can be used as a reference in the `SpecRunner.html` file to replace all existing application code references. The same treatment can be applied to test specifications themselves, but we will not explore this option. We have now two Gulp tasks available and we can execute them together by running the command line:

```
gulp build-app build-tests
```

To view the example web page and execute the tests, we still need to open two HTML files manually in the browser, and this should be something that we can automate. Thanks to the plugin called gulp-open, we can define two new tasks that will open the required HTML files after we execute the following command line:

```
npm install gulp-open --save-dev
```

These are the two new tasks definitions in `gulpfile.js`:

```
var open = require('gulp-open');
gulp.task('open-app', ['build-app'], function() {
  gulp.src('./index.html')
    .pipe(open());
});
gulp.task('open-tests', ['build-tests'], function() {
```

```
gulp.src('./SpecRunner.html')
  .pipe(open({
    app: 'firefox'
  }));
});
```

Both tasks depend on the task that created the bundles and the first one opens the HTML file using the default application for this type of file, while the second task sets a specific application identifier to open the HTML file. (More details about the gulp-open API can be found at https://www.npmjs.com/package/gulp-open). Executing the following command will create the test application code bundle and open the SpecRunner.html file in Mozilla Firefox, where all the test specification will be executed automatically:

gulp open-tests

There are other plugins that can execute the test specifications in the background and display the results in the Gulp console log or in a designated file, but we will not cover them here.

We can now define the default task as an empty task that depends on the two top-level tasks we defined earlier:

```
gulp.task('default', ['open-app', 'open-tests'], function() {
});
```

When we execute the gulp command, the two bundle files will be build and the two HTML files will be opened in the browser.

 We can easily define a watch task triggered on file changes that can remove the need to execute Gulp manually. For this type of task and many others, please see https://github.com/gulpjs/gulp/blob/master/docs/recipes/README.md.

Reusing code based on Underscore between client and server

One of the biggest advantages of using JavaScript for client-server applications is the possibility of code reuse between the two environments. For example, one can easily envisage a validation utility that could be used to validate data on the client and then again on the server. Class definitions are another good example of code that can be reused.

Before ES6, JavaScript did not have any built-in concept of code encapsulation or modularization, unlike other languages such as Java, C#, or Ruby. ES6 solves this problem by standardizing modules and classes, but stops short of standardizing a module loader. A separate ECMAScript module loader specification is under development and published at `http://whatwg.github.io/loader/`, and this specification tries to reconcile browser and Node.js module systems among other goals. Currently, there is at least one working implementation of a module loader that tracks this specification, and it is available at `https://github.com/ModuleLoader/es6-module-loader`.

There are package managers such as jspm (`http://jspm.io`) that enable ES6 modules in the browser and can reference other ES6, CommonJS, and AMD modules, or even regular JavaScript files that are using global variables to provide their functionality.

Rather than focusing on a specific environment, we will use a workflow that allows us to reuse modules between client and server environments, and we will start with revisiting the module system used by Node.js.

Using CommonJS modules for packaging client code with Browserify

Node.js implements the CommonJS module specification, and through its npm package manager, you have access to an extensive number of modules that is not yet matched (even by far) by any other JavaScript package managers. When you compare the CommonJS and the ES6 module systems, you will find they are very similar. In some respect, the ES6 module system looks like a redesign of CommonJS, and transpilers such as Babel can easily convert ES6 modules to CommonJS modules, as discussed previously.

Many of the frontend packages such as jQuery and Bootstrap (for which we used browser-targeted package managers such as Bower) are also available as npm packages. Underscore has an npm package that will detect the environment where it is deployed, and will register itself as a global variable or a CommonJS module accordingly. Due to the abundance and popularity of npm packages, there are tools that can transform CommonJS modules into special packages that can run in the browser. One of the more popular such tools is Browserify (`http://browserify.org`).

Browserify is a bundling tool that transforms CommonJS modules into code that can run in the browser, in the process preventing any potential name clashes or global scope pollution. Browserify relies on the fact that many Node.js modules published on npm can also work on the browser without any change. For the ones that don't, Browserify provides its own implementation of many built-in Node.js libraries, such as buffer, console, crypto, and stream, to name just a few. As long as a module does not use server I/O, there are great chances that it could run in the browser via the Browserify compatibility layer.

The Browserify CLI process usually takes a JavaScript file as a starting point and another JavaScript file as a target for the resulting bundle. Browserify uses logic similar to the Node.js module loader and will identify all dependent modules starting from the initial source file, packaging them up in a bundle that is self sufficient, and in which each initial CommonJS module is uniquely identified. To understand why Browserify is useful, we will start exploring a series of examples without going too much into its inner details. You can find out more details about Browserify and how it works by reading its excellent official handbook at `https://github.com/substack/browserify-handbook`.

We will start by converting the code from the previous example found in the `gulp-automation` folder into a Browserify ready example. The first step is to replace all existing Bower packages with their npm equivalent by removing the `bower_components` folder, the `bower.json` file and then running the following commands:

```
npm install --save jquery
npm install --save bootstrap
npm install --save underscore
```

We will now proceed and change all the files from the `app` folder (and rename the `index.js` to `index_client.js`) to their CommonJS equivalent. This process is identical to the one used in *Chapter 5, Using Underscore.js in the Browser, on the Server, and with the Database,* and the required files can be copied from the `nodejs-underscore` folder from the source code for that chapter. We will also copy the `index.js` file from there to `app/index_server.js` in our current example. We now have a Node.js baseline that can be used as a reference for the code that we will package for the browser shortly. If we run the following command line, we should see the same output as seen in the previous chapter:

```
node app/index_server.js
```

We can now transform the `index_client.js` file into a CommonJS friendly version and the first thing we need to do is import jQuery as a Node.js module. This is made possible by the fact that we are using jQuery 2 that has built in support for the Node.js environment. Most of the contents of the `index_client.js` file remain unchanged, with the exception of the require statements:

```
var $ = require('jquery');
var _ = require("underscore");
var clientRetriever = require("./clientRetriever.js");
var transformations = require("./transformations.js");
$(function() {
  var oldestClients = clientRetriever.getOldestClients(5);
  ...
  onSelectHome();
});
```

Notice that we use the short form of the `jQuery.ready()` function, and we reference all former global variables such as `clientRetriever` and `transformations` as CommonJS modules. At this point, we can use Browserify to prepare the client bundle, and we will install it as a global npm module first:

npm install --global browserify

The next step is to execute Browserify, specifying the entry point file as the first argument and the output file as the second:

browserify app/index_client.js --outfile public/app.js

Looking at the newly generated file, `public/app.js`, you will notice that each individual module that can be traced back from `index_client.js` is concatenated and wrapped into a function body, including jQuery and Underscore source files. To check whether the resulting bundle has maintained its functionality, we will modify the `index.html` file and reference the `public/app.js` output file instead of all previous JavaScript file references. We also need to point the Bootstrap style sheet to its new `node_modules` location, and you should be able to see a working example when you open the `index.html` file in a browser. You can find the current example in the `gulp-browserify` folder from the source code for this chapter.

> Browserify has support for generating multiple bundles and referencing modules from different bundles. For example, you can create a bundle for external libraries and one for application code. Browserify also has support for source maps that make it easier to identify the original code during debugging in a browser that supports source maps. You can find more about the Browserify API and CLI at `https://github.com/substack/node-browserify`.

Testing CommonJS modules in the browser with Browserify

We can take the CommonJS module transformation further and convert the test specifications to CommonJS modules. These are similar to the ones found in the `nodejs-underscore/spec` folder from the source code for *Chapter 5, Using Underscore.js in the Browser, on the Server, and with the Database*. Next, we will apply the same commands from the previous chapter to set up the example folder for running Node.js tests via the Jasmine CLI:

```
npm install --global jasmine
jasmine init
```

The `spec` folder containing the Jasmine configuration file `spec/support/jasmine.json` should now be created, and if we copy the CommonJS test specifications, we can execute them by calling `jasmine` in the command line from the `gulp-browserify` example folder.

We have executed the server side Node.js tests, and thanks to Browserify, we can also execute the same tests in a browser environment. First, we need to generate the test specifications bundle via the following command:

```
browserify spec/*Spec.js --outfile spec/output/specs.js
```

Notice that we specified multiple entry point files as the first argument while keeping a single file as output. The generated file contains all the source code and test specifications wrapped as Browserify client compatible modules.

We no longer have Jasmine available as a Bower package, but we can install its npm equivalent, the `jasmine-core` library that contains the required files to execute the tests in the browser:

```
npm install jasmine-core --save-dev
```

We will modify the `SpecRunner.html` file and add the Jasmine `node_modules` references and replace all code and test specifications links with one link to the `spec/output/specs.js` file:

```
<!DOCTYPE HTML>
<html>
<head>
  <meta http-equiv="Content-Type" content="text/html;
  charset=UTF-8">
```

```
<title>Jasmine Spec Runner v2.3.4</title>

<link rel="shortcut icon" type="image/png"
href="node_modules/jasmine-core/images/jasmine_favicon.png">
<link rel="stylesheet" type="text/css"
href="node_modules/jasmine-core/lib/jasmine-core/jasmine.css">

<script type="text/javascript" src="node_modules/jasmine-
core/lib/jasmine-core/jasmine.js"></script>
<script type="text/javascript" src="node_modules/jasmine-
core/lib/jasmine-core/jasmine-html.js"></script>
<script type="text/javascript" src="node_modules/jasmine-
core/lib/jasmine-core/boot.js"></script>

<!-- include source files here... -->
<!-- include spec files here... -->
<script type="text/javascript"
src="spec/output/specs.js"></script>
</head>
<body>
</body>
</html>
```

If we open this file in any cross platform browser such as Google Chrome or Mozilla Firefox, we should see all tests passing. We now have both code and tests that run on the server and in the browser using Node.js and Browserify.

Using Gulp with Browserify

Working directly with the Browserify CLI is a great way to learn this tool, but it does not suit an automated build scenario. Browserify is versatile and can be loaded as a Node.js module in a server file such as the `gulpfile.js` file used to automate the build process via Gulp.

First, we need to install Browserify as an npm package local to our `gulp-browserify` example folder so that we can start using it as a module and access its API:

npm install browserify --save-dev

The output stream from the Browserify API is not compatible with the streams expected by Gulp, so we will install the package `vinyl-source-stream` (`https://github.com/hughsk/vinyl-source-stream`) that makes the necessary conversion:

npm install vinyl-source-stream --save-dev

We can now update the Gulp task `build-app` to use the newly installed npm package:

```
var gulp = require('gulp');
var browserify = require('browserify');
var source = require('vinyl-source-stream');
gulp.task('build-app', function() {
    return browserify('./app/index_client.js')
        .bundle()
        .pipe(source('app.js'))
        .pipe(gulp.dest('./public/'));
});
```

The first line of the task initializes the Browserify instance with the entry point file and the subsequent call to `bundle()` returns a readable stream. This readable stream is then converted to the type of Node.js stream expected by Gulp via the `source()` call.

When we execute the following command, we should end up with the same file generated via the Browserify CLI at `public/app.js`:

gulp build-app

In order to modify the Gulp task `build-test` to use Browserify, we need to rely on the glob module to load the entry point files representing the test specifications. We have to install it first as an npm package:

npm install glob --save-dev

The Gulp task `build-tests` will use the `glob.sync()` method to search for test specifications and returns an array of matching file names. The Browserify API supports initialization from an array of file names and our Gulp task is now changed to this:

```
var gulp = require('gulp');
var glob = require('glob');
var browserify = require('browserify');
var source = require('vinyl-source-stream');
gulp.task('build-tests', function() {
    var specFiles = glob.sync('./spec/**/*Spec.js');
    return browserify({
        entries: specFiles
    })
    .bundle()
```

```
    .pipe(source('specs.js'))
    .pipe(gulp.dest('./spec/output/'));
});
```

Executing the following command will generate the same bundled test specification file at the `spec/output/specs.js` location that we generated with the Browserify API:

gulp bundle-tests

All the intermediary tasks now run synchronously as the task functions return an object. The reason for this change in behavior is due to Browserify being slower than the previous concatenation actions. If the task is run asynchronously, we might end up with the browser being launched while the output file is still being built, and the tests will fail because of that. If we execute the `gulp` executable, we should have the same output with the one from the `gulp-automation` folder, while relying on reusable CommonJS modules that can be referenced in Node.js and in the browser.

 You can find more details about the Gulp and Browserify integration, including links to more comprehensive Gulp examples at the blog entry `https://viget.com/extend/gulp-browserify-starter-faq`.

Adding ECMAScript 2015 (ES6) support to Browserify

When we explored Babel's capabilities, we looked at a key feature where by default Babel will transpile ES6 modules as CommonJS modules that can be loaded natively by Node.js. Because Browserify also supports CommonJS files, we could write code using the ES6 module syntax, transpile it via Babel into CommonJS modules, and then use Browserify to create a bundle that can run in the browser.

Browserify has extensive supports for plugins and transformations that add extra functionality that is not provided by default. Browserify can apply a transformation to its source files before they are processed for bundling. One such transformer called babelify can convert ES6 modules to CommonJS modules via the Babel API.

Before we modify our Gulp tasks to use this new transformer, we will follow a similar workflow to the previous subsection. Before we build the browser bundles, we will create an ES6 baseline codebase that can be exercised and tested via the `babel-node` and `jasmine-es6` executables.

In the process, we will make minimal changes to make the code ES6 compatible: use the new module syntax, arrow functions, classes, and change all converted files to end with the .es6 extension to make it obvious that we are working with ES6 code.

You can find the example in the gulp-browserify-es6 folder from the source code for this folder, and we will include the app/index_server.es6 file as an example of the converted ES6 code:

```
import _ from "underscore";
import * as clientRetriever from "./clientRetriever.es6";
import * as transformations from "./transformations.es6";
var oldestClients = clientRetriever.getOldestClients(5);
var bestClients = clientRetriever.getBestClients(5);
var clients = clientRetriever.getClients();
console.log("There are " + clients.length + " clients.");
var getContactsOutput = (clients) => {
  var outputText = "";
  _.forEach(clients, (client, index) => {
    if (index > 0) {
      outputText += ", ";
    }
    outputText += transformations.getContactNameIdAndType(client);
  });
  return outputText;
};
console.log("Top 5 oldest clients with name, id and type: " +
getContactsOutput(oldestClients));
console.log("Top 5 best clients with name, id and type: " +
getContactsOutput(bestClients));
```

Executing the following command should output the same console messages as the example from the previous subsection:

babel-node app/index_server.es6

If we install the jasmine-es6 npm package via the following command, we will be able to execute ES6 tests using its CLI:

npm install jasmine-es6 --save-dev

If the file spec/support/jasmine.json matches the following code snippet, we can execute the tests using the node_modules/.bin/jasmine command:

```
{
  "spec_dir": "spec",
  "spec_files": [
```

```
      "**/*[sS]pec.js",
      "**/*[sS]pec.es6"
    ],
    "helpers": [
      "../node_modules/jasmine-es6/lib/install.js",
      "helpers/**/*.js"
    ]
  }
```

We will now convert the `index_client.js` file to ES6 and start modifying the Gulp tasks to bundle ES6 modules via babelify and Browserify. First, let's install babelify as a development npm package:

npm install --save-dev babelify

The Gulp task `build-app` was changed to use babelify:

```
var gulp = require('gulp');
var browserify = require('browserify');
var source = require('vinyl-source-stream');
var babelify = require('babelify');
gulp.task('build-app', function() {
  return browserify('./app/index_client.es6')
    .transform(babelify)
    .bundle()
    .pipe(source('app.js'))
    .pipe(gulp.dest('./public/'));
});
```

Notice how we applied the babelify transform before creating the bundle and a similar approach can be observed in the `build-tests` task. Executing the gulp command in the current example folder `gulp-browserify-es6` will have the expected outcome: the `index.html` will display correctly and all the tests executed in `SpecRunner.html` should pass.

Summary

In this chapter, we explored Gulp: a build automation tool that simplifies deployments. The last major topic of the book was on how to reuse JavaScript code between client and server environments, and we identified Browserify as a key tool that makes CommonJS modules executable in the browser. The final section presented a workflow where ES6 modules can be reused between client and server via Browserify and babelify.

Index

Thank you for buying
Learning Underscore.js

About Packt Publishing

Packt, pronounced 'packed', published its first book, *Mastering phpMyAdmin for Effective MySQL Management*, in April 2004, and subsequently continued to specialize in publishing highly focused books on specific technologies and solutions.

Our books and publications share the experiences of your fellow IT professionals in adapting and customizing today's systems, applications, and frameworks. Our solution-based books give you the knowledge and power to customize the software and technologies you're using to get the job done. Packt books are more specific and less general than the IT books you have seen in the past. Our unique business model allows us to bring you more focused information, giving you more of what you need to know, and less of what you don't.

Packt is a modern yet unique publishing company that focuses on producing quality, cutting-edge books for communities of developers, administrators, and newbies alike. For more information, please visit our website at www.packtpub.com.

About Packt Open Source

In 2010, Packt launched two new brands, Packt Open Source and Packt Enterprise, in order to continue its focus on specialization. This book is part of the Packt Open Source brand, home to books published on software built around open source licenses, and offering information to anybody from advanced developers to budding web designers. The Open Source brand also runs Packt's Open Source Royalty Scheme, by which Packt gives a royalty to each open source project about whose software a book is sold.

Writing for Packt

We welcome all inquiries from people who are interested in authoring. Book proposals should be sent to author@packtpub.com. If your book idea is still at an early stage and you would like to discuss it first before writing a formal book proposal, then please contact us; one of our commissioning editors will get in touch with you.

We're not just looking for published authors; if you have strong technical skills but no writing experience, our experienced editors can help you develop a writing career, or simply get some additional reward for your expertise.

PUBLISHING

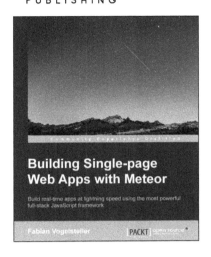

Building Single-page Web Apps with Meteor

ISBN: 978-1-78398-812-9   Paperback: 198 pages

Build real-time apps at lightning speed using the most powerful full-stack JavaScript framework

1. Create a complete web blog from frontend to backend that uses only JavaScript.

2. Understand how Web 2.0 is made by powerful browser-based applications.

3. Step-by-step tutorial that will show you how fast, complex web applications can be built.

Getting Started with Gulp

ISBN: 978-1-78439-576-6   Paperback: 120 pages

Create powerful automations with gulp to improve the efficiency of your web project workflow

1. Learn the basics of Node.js, npm, and gulp and how they work together.

2. Harness the power of gulp to solve a number of recurring problems that you are likely to face while building complex web applications.

3. A step-by-step guide to help you simplify and manage complex tasks such as image compression, minification, and so on.